GENE W. MASON

PRENTICE-HALL, INC.
ENGLEWOOD CLIFFS, N. J.

MINUS THREE

MINUS THREE by Gene W. Mason
© 1970 by Gene W. Mason
Copyright under International and Pan American
Copyright Conventions
All rights reserved. No part of this book may be
reproduced in any form or by any means, except
for the inclusion of brief quotations in a review,
without permission in writing from the publisher.
Library of Congress Catalog Card Number: 74-124316
Printed in the United States of America T
ISBN-0-13-584714-1
Prentice-Hall International, Inc., London
Prentice-Hall of Australia, Pty. Ltd., Sydney
Prentice-Hall of Canada, Ltd., Toronto
Prentice-Hall of India Private Ltd., New Delhi
Prentice-Hall of Japan, Inc., Tokyo

This
book is
dedicated to
those who wait in
the valleys, worrying
and wondering, but never
quite understanding why their
loved ones trod the summits.

Foreword

MINUS THREE is not another book on the glories of mountaineering. It is not, as are so many books on the subject, even particularly philosophical. Dr. Gene Mason tells a casually frank and at times joltingly honest story of men striving against great mountains. Not heroes of legend, but ordinary people driven by extraordinary motivation.

Adventure there is in plenty, but more striking is the insight provided into the minds and actions of the climbers themselves. Dr. Mason brings out his petty thoughts as well as his profound ones, his mistakes as well as his triumphs. Expedition planning is at times sketchy and decisions are made that are at best questionable. Yet from all this comes a picture which my own background in ice climbing tells me is much more real than the ones found in some of the classic tales of mountaineering.

I am often reminded of similarities between Dr. Mason's experiences in the mountains and my early career in deep diving. Both environments are hostile to man. Both can be numbingly cold and capriciously dispense winds of air or water which may carry one to disaster. Too little air in the heights or too much in the depths produce a similar deterioration of mental capacity. Regardless of the hazards and discomforts, though, people still climb high and they still dive deep. There is a lure that brings some of us back again and again.

Why? There is more involved than the diver's high pay or the climber's few moments on a dramatic summit. More also than the occasional exhilaration that one meets going up or down. Challenge is certainly important, but for many that sense of challenge is only a symptom of something far deeper.

I do not know the ultimate answer. Gene Mason does not provide it in *Minus Three*. But the picture he paints takes us part of the way. It outlines in stark perspective the almost involuntary determination of Dr. Mason and his comrades in the face of incredible hardships and appalling chances.

Jon W. Lindbergh

▲

Introduction

Most men slip into the stream of life, and follow a rather narrow channel banked by the conventions and rules of society. Some sink to the bottom, some rise to the surface, but most follow the same general course.

A few men during their lifetime are able to deviate significantly from this rigid course, and yet still find their way back into the mainstream. This book is about three such deviations from the main course of life—the challenging of the summits of three of the continents of the world.

The Western Hemisphere is formed by the North and South American continents and the Central American bridge between them. The highest point on each of these continents is the culmination of hundreds of square miles of desolate, snow-covered, glacier-strewn granite—20,320-foot Mount McKinley in Alaska and 23,000-foot Mount Aconcagua in Argentina.

While the advance of civilization has changed the face of the world, these great citadels have changed little through the centuries. Thus, Dr. Frederick Cook's 1904 description of Mount McKinley is almost as appropriate today as it was some sixty years ago: "The area of this mountain is far inland, in the heart of a most difficult and trackless country, making the transportation of men and supplies a very arduous task. The thick underbrush, the endless marshes, and the myriads of vicious mosquitoes bring to the traveler the troubles of the tropics; the necessity of fording and swimming icy streams, the almost perpetual cold rains, the camps in high altitudes on glaciers, in snows and violent storms, bring to the traveler all the discomforts of the arctic explorer; the very difficult slopes, combined with high altitude effects, add the troubles of the worst Alpine climbs. The prospective conqueror of America's culminating peak will be amply rewarded, but he must be prepared to withstand the tortures of the torrids, the discomforts of the North Pole seeker, combined with the hardships of the Matterhorn ascent multiplied many times."

The South Americans have a term they apply to the conquerors of Mount Aconcagua— "*hombre mucho*, much man." Mount Aconcagua has claimed more lives than any major mountain in the Western Hemisphere. Thirty-four victims have died on its slopes, although many books list the unofficial number as over one hundred.

Ernest Hemingway in his famous short story, "The Snows of Kilimanjaro," introduced much of the world to his favorite mountain, and the third mountain challenged in this book, with the following description: "Kilimanjaro is a snow covered mountain 19,710 feet high, and is said to be the highest mountain in Africa. Its western summit is called the Masai 'Ngàje Ngài,' the House of God. Close to the western summit there is the dried and frozen carcass of a leopard. No one has explained what the leopard was seeking at that altitude."

The conquest of the summits of three continents is as many as any man has ever achieved. The original goal was to challenge all seven continents, but time has a way of eroding strength, opportunity, and enthusiasm.

It is my sincere hope that this book will stimulate a few men to explore some of the side channels in life, or at least to have compassion for those who do.

CONTENTS

Part Three ▲ KILIMANJARO

MC KINLEY

1 ▲
OVERLAND APPROACH

IT WAS VERY cold. We quickly unloaded our equipment and watched the two vehicles, our last contact with civilization, disappear into the grayness. An incredible feeling of loneliness swept me. The time was after midnight, but during June in the land of the midnight sun, a dusklike light blankets the land throughout the night. I looked over the snow-covered hills in the direction of the summit, and wondered what hazards we would encounter in the seventy miles between us. Seventy miles. We had anticipated only thirty-five, but heavy snows and a late Spring had made the roads impassable. It was a bitter disappointment. Until some of the food and fuel was consumed, our packs would have to weigh nearly seventy pounds. I was already beginning to dread hoisting mine onto my back in the morning.

As I crawled into my sleeping bag my mind wandered over the last couple of days. It was little more than yesterday that we had said goodbye to our friends and family. Goodbyes are painful things at best, and after leaving I always have the feeling that I didn't say what I wanted to. But I had said what I could and we were winging our way northward full of hope and apprehension for the great adventure. The following morning at three we had left Anchorage by car caravan, covering the three hundred miles to Mount McKinley National Park. I had been struck by the contrast between the highly civilized machines that transported us and the almost medieval adventure we were undertaking—attempting to storm a castle of ice and rock surrounded by the coldest and swiftest moats.

Our weapons would be ropes, axes, metal hardware, and physical strength.

I had dressed in the early morning and was sitting, sleepy-eyed, trying to dispel that morning logginess. I sipped a cup of hot chocolate and looked at our six-member team, thinking of how and why we had come together.

It's strange that I can't remember when I decided to climb the mountain. Perhaps it's easier to answer why. Every man has a spark of adventure buried within him, covered by the burdens of civilization, responsibility, and conformity. In some men the spark never does more than smolder, while in others, perhaps not buried as deeply, it is fanned to brightness by his surroundings and companions, and finally bursts forth into a bright flame.

This spark of adventure causes a man to seriously consider climbing a mountain, but the final decision is under the influence of other factors. In the final analysis, each man has his own private reason for wanting to reach the summit of a great mountain. The reasons he'll give will sometimes be clever, more often trite, but rarely the truth.

A thirty-three-year-old doctor of medicine, I wondered exactly what had finally motivated me. I looked up from my swirling hot chocolate toward my teammates. Uniformly the faces had a look of seriousness, but each was quick to break into a nervous smile when my eyes met theirs.

While none of us were especially large, Ralph Mackey at 139 pounds was the smallest. His small features peered at me through glasses from within his bulky red parka. The expedition had been conceived by Ralph, who was my age, and myself, and gradually we enlisted the others. He became our treasurer and public relations man. A small nonscientific expedition must necessarily be financed by the members. This adds an additional stress. Proper publicity and the right contacts allow a certain amount of discount and sometimes some supplies are donated. It was Ralph who arranged our official title, The Century 21 Mount McKinley Expedition 1962, in connection with the Seattle World's Fair. We were given the Exposition flag to place on the summit.

As Ralph opened his pack this morning, a small teddy bear dropped out. Naturally we accused him of carrying it for security while he mumbled embarassedly about being sabotaged by his own kids. Ralph is the sales manager of his family-owned stove works, and an only child. He had been considered a sickly youngster, and had spent the better part of his manhood attempting to dispel a reputation of fragility.

I glanced at Kenn Carpenter, also thirty-three years old. He was analytically stirring his steaming hot cereal like the engineer that he was. The rising steam occasionally fogged his glasses for a second. Ralph and I had asked Kenn to be our climb leader. A more experienced climber than either of us, he had led an unsuccessful assault on Mount McKinley four years before. He had led his party onto the Muldrow Glacier, only to find a recent earthquake had transformed it into miles of huge impassable seracs and crevasses. The disheartened group had trudged home. He had always wondered whether, with a little more daring and foresight, he might have been able to by-pass this area and ascend by way of one of the ridges.

Kenn had chosen our equipment and food with great care. The far north location of Mount McKinley's 20,320-foot summit may well present the most severe year-round climate of any spot on earth. The equipment was chosen so as to provide the necessities of life through a thirty-day polar expedition in three dimensions. It weighed about 550 pounds.

The food had to be lightweight, resistant to spoilage, and palatable, since appetites tend to fade at altitude. The problem of how much food to carry was solved in the following manner. We knew that mountaineering requires about five thousand calories per day in order to maintain body weight. The lowest weight consistent with five thousand calories, and still palatable, was found to be about two-and-a-half to three pounds. For thirty days we needed ninety pounds of food per man, 540 pounds for the expedition.

Since our total supply weight was close to eleven hundred pounds, or over 180 pounds per man, we arranged for an air-drop of seven hundred pounds at 7200 feet altitude. Federal regulations in the Park allow only *one* air drop at a specified limit in altitude. We spent many days meticulously packaging our food to withstand shipping abuse, rodent attack, spoilage, and a free fall of a hundred feet or more onto an icy glacier. We had shipped our equipment and food to Alaska a month in advance of our departure, but now I was beginning to wonder if we could snowshoe to the airdrop site by the specified date, since the distance had been doubled by the late arrival of a spring thaw. I knew that more than one expedition had failed because they weren't able to receive their airdrop.

Jon Hisey was bent over our stove dishing up a bowl of cereal. He had been the first one out of his sleeping bag, and had gotten the kerosene burner into action. Jon, a thirty-eight-year-old line foreman for the telephone company, had accompanied Kenn four years previously on the unsuccessful Mount McKinley climb.

One of the tasks we had assigned to him was to organize a master repair kit, capable of repairing any piece of expedition equipment. A broken ice axe, snowshoe, or stove could cost us the summit, as could a tear in a tent or a rubber boot. An item that may be easily repaired with a piece of wire, tape, or some small part may be impossible to repair without it. Nothing can be safely overlooked.

Jon, our oldest member and a bachelor, was one of the eldest sons in a large family. Raised in the Northwest in pioneer simplicity, he learned early the necessity of combined human effort for comfortable existence. He had a strong influence on our team both physically and psychologically.

At twenty-six, Ron Muecke was the youngest member of our group. His clean-cut appearance was beginning to disappear behind a layer of black stubble spreading over his cheeks and chin. Since he was a computer technician at a large aircraft company, he was given the job of determining whether gas or liquid fuel would be the heaviest, and which would be the least expensive. He decided that kerosene stoves, primed with alcohol, would be best suited for our expedition. The next logical question was how much fuel to carry for a six-man, thirty-day expedition. Above five thousand feet all of our water would have to be derived from melting snow. Besides what we would need for drinking, water would be necessary for putting dehydrated foods into solution. I explained human fluid requirements, we determined the water necessary to rehydrate foods, and we calculated the number of calories needed to convert ice into water. Then Ron poured the information into one of his computers. The answer was thirteen gallons of kerosene and three quarts of priming alcohol.

Ron had a degree from a good university, but somehow his postgraduate plans had gone astray and he had been forced by necessity into unskilled employment. Given these conditions, he was intensely anxious to excel. His wife was pregnant with their firstborn when we began planning our expedition. She had delivered a few weeks before our departure. I knew that thoughts of his wife and child caused him mixed emotions about our climb.

I couldn't help but smile when I looked at the last member to join our expedition. She quickly smiled back, her pretty, freckled face framed by short blond hair protruding from the edges of her parka. Recruiting the last member of our expedition had taken many months. Repeatedly individuals would join us, eventually become disenchanted with the training, logistics, or potential hazards, and drop out. We hadn't asked Helen Niblock, because early in our planning we had decided to exclude women because of the rather obvious difficulties involved. However, we had come to the point where we felt it wise to reconsider, since we had exhausted our supply of qualified male mountaineers. Helen had been fairly active in mountaineering for about three years. We decided to accept her as a member if she would join us.

Helen, an extremely capable surgical nurse, was thirty-three years old and unmarried. This expedition represented a certain special fulfillment to her, and she joined us immediately when we suggested it to her.

I finished my hot chocolate and warmed my hands on the empty cup. I knew that to a very large extent the success or failure of a mountain assault was determined before departure by the adequacy of planning and by the interplay of personalities and plans. A mountain assault team must be selected with the care given to the selection of a submarine crew. I wondered if we were of the proper temperament to undergo the inevitable hardships while living continuously within a few feet of each other. A sense of humor would certainly help.

Breakfast was over. We divided the loads into six piles and jammed our packs full; all extra items were placed in a duffel bag and tied to an extension on top of the frame. Among other things, I was carrying the expedition medical kit. Its preparation had required a careful calculation that took into consideration weight, freezing, and breakage of drugs, and the probable occurrence of various maladies. Undoubtedly some eventualities would find us short on supplies, so I attempted to be ready for the expected, and ready to improvise for the unexpected. Certainly a large mishap would bring the expedition to a halt, but if members could be treated fairly effectively and be kept on the move, a potential failure could be turned into a success.

Squatting down, I fastened on my snowshoes. I set my teeth and tried to swing the huge pack onto my back. In spite of much grunting and straining I couldn't do it. Embarrassed, I looked up to see if my companions were having the same difficulty. They were, and I felt somewhat relieved. We helped each other on with the packs and began crunching across the snow-covered tundra. The weight was oppressive. I thought of the three months of punishing physical conditioning, consisting primarily of running: running up stairs, running to the store, running home, running until overcome by gasping exhaustion, and then running some more. Running sometimes with dogs chasing and people pointing, but running just the same. Before departing we were all able to run six miles nonstop in one hour. It occurred to me that we hadn't trained enough.

After the sting of the first day passed, it seemed that we were shuffling along endlessly over hills, down valleys, across rivers, and through huge expanses of willow marsh. It was essential that we cover sixty miles in four days in order to be present for our scheduled air drop on the glacier at seven thousand feet. If we weren't there the pilot wouldn't drop the supplies, and our expedition would come to an end almost before it started.

While moving across the tundra, we came upon several sets of antlers not yet devoured by the rodents who use them as a calcium source. Often we came upon caribou awkwardly galloping out of our way as we plodded onward. Trapped gases, such as those in the intestine, unfortunately expand some 50 percent in going from sea level to ten thousand feet. As we gained altitude it was reassuring to be able to blame unpleasant odors on "those damn caribou following us again."

2 ▲
On the Glacier

Our six-member team moved slowly up the mountain. Our party had started at the base of the mountain six days ago. We had covered sixty of the seventy miles to the summit, but only a few thousand vertical feet of the almost four-mile-high mountain. We were now on the great Muldrow Glacier, approaching the Lower Ice Fall—the glacier that had defied all attempts to climb it for the past five years. At that time an earthquake had broken it into a waterless sea of impassable icebergs.

Our two rope teams cautiously picked their way among the grotesque ice forms. As hundreds of feet of snow build up on the mountain through the years, the enormous weight compresses the lower levels to solid ice. With continued pressure the ice is finally set into motion until it becomes a river of ice flowing down the mountain like a layer of frosting flowing over a mound of cake. As the rigid ice layer passes over an irregularity it cracks. These gigantic cracks are called crevasses, and they are produced in wild profusion as the glacier flows over and around protrusions and depressions on the rocky walls and base of the cirque valleys. Although these huge rivers of ice have been known to flow as rapidly as two hundred feet a day, they usually flow only inches a day. The crevasses vary in width from a few inches to a hundred feet or more. They often extend all the way down to the base rock, two hundred to four hundred feet below—the height of a twenty- or forty-story building.

Kenn, our climb leader, was putting in the route. He would

take several steps, thrust our eight-foot bamboo probing pole into the snow ahead of him, withdraw it, take a couple more steps, make another thrust, and so forth. This exhausting task is essential for uncovering the hidden crevasses, a maze of traps awaiting the careless climber. Snow freezes across the crevasses, sometimes scant inches thick, sometimes several feet thick. The probing provides an indication of the depth of these snow bridges. A misleading thrust, an inept judgment, a collapse of the bridge means a plunge into the seemingly bottomless frozen pit.

I was sixty feet behind Kenn, connected to him by a nylon rope. Occasionally I felt tugs from Ron, connected sixty feet behind me. Even though physically connected in this manner we seldom got any closer, because to concentrate ourselves over a small area would expose us to the hazards of the likely collapse of the terrain surface. I shuffled along with my snowshoes in Kenn's tracks, watching his progress closely. My ice axe was tensely poised. If he should plummet into a crevasse, the depth of his fall would be directly proportional to my speed and efficiency in effecting an ice axe self-arrest. This technique is performed by slamming the pick of the axe into the ice while the other hand grips the shaft diagonally across the chest. In this manner a slide is arrested.

I began counting my steps—five, six, seven—somehow counting helped me forget the fifty-five-pound pack that burned into my shoulders. Sixty-three, sixty-four, sixty-five—it also gave me some indication as to when the next few seconds rest would occur. Fatigue increased with each step, until you wondered how you would take another, but another step you took. Two hundred three, two hundred four—the rope slackened as Kenn stuck the probing pole into the snow and leaned over in a standing position, resting his pack on a ski pole. Our rest had begun. As I bent from the waist to lean my pack onto my poles, the perspiration dripped from my hair and face, cascading off my nose into the snow. On a cloudless day there is almost no escape from the fiery sun. The rays bounce off the snow and burn the inside of the nose and ears. Lips crack and bleed after a few days. The heavy protective sun creams are washed off with perspiration. There is only one shelter, I thought, as I looked into a deep glacial chasm of blue ice. The crevasses call like a Lorelei—but they won't have us. I gritted my teeth almost painfully. The rope tensed and I looked up at Kenn. He slowly assumed an erect posture, squinted up at the mountain through his dark tinted goggles, and resumed his probing.

I started counting again—three, four, five—I was thinking about the crevasse training we had undergone in a shady backyard. We had hung from a rope attached high in a tree and had ascended the rope by means of prussik slings. As I thought about this my hand automatically was checking the three slings knotted into my rope—one sling around the chest to avoid hanging upside down, one sling for the left foot, and one for the right, each of them knotted into the climbing rope with a prussik knot that holds under tension and slides when relaxed. By standing in alternate slings and sliding the slack sling, a vertical rope can be ascended, and escape from a crevasse becomes possible.

We penetrated farther into the Lower Ice Fall, surrounded by the broken walls of great towering masses of snow-covered ice. Suddenly I set my feet as a muffled rumble shook the ice under us. I felt a wave of goose bumps run up my arms into my neck. The glacier had just moved, only a half inch perhaps, but enough to give the impression that the earth was about to swallow us up. We resumed our methodical pace.

The glacier was becoming more and more distorted and broken, and Kenn's route progressively more difficult to establish. We were walking through glacial debris that resembled a destroyed snow-covered village after an avalanche. Kenn stopped. Further exploration was considered too hazardous to pursue with snowshoes and heavy packs. We had discussed the likelihood of dropping into a crevasse and having the pack weight snap our necks when we reached the end of the rope. Kenn, Ron, and I would attempt to put in a route.

If "it went," we would return for our packs and snowshoes. Our other rope team settled down in the snow.

Kenn began the interminable probing. My mind began to wander. I was shaken back to reality by a slackening of the rope. This time it was not for a rest. Kenn was preparing to jump a crevasse. He carefully probed the edge for a footing, and then looked back to see if I was in readiness. I waved my assent. His body shifted forward and backward a few times, and then he leaped. A shower of snow filled the air as he landed. He resumed his probing, moving slowly forward.

When I came to the edge of the crevasse I carefully studied his foot prints and gazed into the icy blue-walled chasm before me. I looked toward Kenn, he signaled his readiness, I glanced over my shoulder at Ron. He waved his hand, he had given me enough free rope for the jump. I bent my knees, braced my feet, and sprang. As I landed I fell, going automatically into a self-arrest with my ice axe. Lying in the snow I turned my head. Ron also was lying in the snow. He had gone into a self-arrest when he saw me falling, not knowing whether or not I was in trouble. I raised a hand and waved him up. We both got to our feet and moved on. When Ron reached the crevasse I tensed myself in expectancy. He jumped it without incident.

We were now out on what appeared to be an island of ice. Kenn was climbing up a steep slope hoping to discover a connection that would lead us farther up the glacier. He was out of vision. If no connection existed, we would have to back-track.

An immense tug yanked me off my feet and tumbled me up the steep slope. A mixture of flailing arms and legs thrashed up the hill for twenty feet before my ice axe finally bit into the rock hard surface. Spread-eagled face down in the snow, I gripped my ice axe and slowly regained my wind. I spit the snow out of my mouth; my ribs ached from the shock, and the rope issued tautly from my waist up the slope and over. "Kenn's down a crevasse," I shouted. The rope tug had not reached Ron. I knew that Kenn had fallen a considerable distance. The shock was the same as standing on a roof and throwing off a 160-pound weight attached by a rope to your waist. I wondered if Kenn was conscious, or even alive for that matter. Ropes have been known to break rib after rib until they secure a hold. "Kenn! Kenn!" I shouted. No response. I envisioned Kenn revolving slowly, like a broken puppet, dangling from the end of my rope.

Kenn had reached the top of the slope and had proceeded over what appeared to be a level field of snow. He was probing with his ice axe, but suddenly he was falling. It had happened so quickly there had been no opportunity to shout a warning.

As he hung there slowly spinning, he extended a foot to the icy wall and the spinning stopped. He watched the shower of snow crystals float past him and finally disappear into the dark depths below. He turned his head. His eyes followed the rope up to the light coming down through a body-sized hole. The rest of the crevasse was snow-covered. He judged the distance to be about twenty feet. He moved his arms and legs, and took a deep breath—everything seemed to work. His ice axe still hung by a safety strap around his wrist. He grabbed the rope and pushed off the wall with his feet. He had spotted an irregular crack in the ice wall which could act as a ledge. He was anxious to take his weight off the rope, because he was worried about the security of my position above. As he came in contact with the wet ice wall, it sucked the heat from his body as if it were a giant icy leech. A violent shiver shook his frame. He knew he couldn't survive long in this freezing dungeon without additional clothing. His parka was becoming saturated with the water that was dripping down from above. Bracing his feet and leaning into the wall, he gave the rope three short jerks in an effort to communicate with me. The tugs were dissipated in the snow and I had no idea he was still conscious.

Meanwhile I had shouted our plight to our other rope team. They were approaching us as rapidly as they could. I now had Ron also belayed, and he was cautiously working his way up the pitch hoping to determine if Kenn was conscious, and to evaluate the extent of the rescue operation.

It was several minutes before Ron's voice broke the tense silence. "He's O.K.," he shouted.

"Can you see him?" I shouted back.

"No, just a field of snow with a small hole in it. I don't want to get too close."

"How far down is he?" I asked.

"He says about twenty feet."

By this time our support rope team had arrived. Ralph and Helen anchored themselves securely while the forward member, Jon, took off his rope and fastened a loop in the end. We had decided to bring Kenn out by the *bilgeri* method, a quicker, less fatiguing method than prussiking. Ron crawled carefully toward the hole. When he got as near as he dared, he shoved the looped rope forward with his ice axe until it fell into the hole. He advanced the rope until he heard a muffled cry from below—"Up rope." He withdrew the rope slightly. "This will be right rope," shouted Ron. He then gave a small tug on the original rope and shouted, "This will be left." He then slipped his ice axe under both ropes to prevent their cutting through the snow.

Kenn was wet and cold. His body was starting to ache from the bruising it had undergone. He slipped his right foot into the lowered loop of the rope and his left into one of his sling ropes. He placed a hand on each rope and shouted. "Up right." Ron relayed his command. Our support team took up the rope a couple feet. "Up left," came the next command. I took up the slack in the unweighted rope while Kenn was standing in the other. "Up right," Ron shouted. Now I was holding Kenn, while our support team shortened their rope.

Fifteen minutes of this activity and Kenn stood on top of the slope, looking down at me. He was shivering, and occasionally his teeth chattered. He looked more weary than I had ever seen him.

"It's good to see you again, Kenn," I said.

His chin quivered. "Thanks."

3 ▲
AIRDROP

A STEADY DISTANT drone crept into my ears and finally ignited my consciousness. Almost simultaneously we all popped our heads out the tent flap. Silhouetted against the northern sky was a dark spot with tiny lights, winging its way up the valley. By the time it was over our camp we were waving and shouting. Kenn had pulled the fuse on a smoke bomb. Like a moth dancing around a flame, the plane darted around the column of red smoke drifting skyward. Determining the wind direction, the plane swooped down to about one hundred feet over the glacier and discharged a tumbling cardboard box with a red streamer. The box bounced in the snow with a couple of thuds. The plane turned, swooped again, and another streamered box took flight. In eighteen climbing, diving, banking, almost stalling passes our eighteen boxes were hurled down to us. The plane then headed back down the valley, and with a waggle of its wings became an ever decreasing speck, the drone of its engine finally disappearing into the heavy silence of the mountain.

The six of us spread out over the glacier and retrieved the parcels. We expected twelve more bundles but we assumed they would be dropped the next morning. Then everyone retired but me. I sat in the snow looking up the valley toward the summit—a dome of pure white, ten miles away, standing out against the gray sky. As I looked about, I was almost startled by the complete lack of color. Everything was white, black, or shades thereof. A color photograph would look almost exactly like a black and white print. The only color was that which we had brought with us—yellow tents, orange or blue parkas, red wands. I felt that we had somehow found it essential to bring color with us, just as we had brought food, fuel, clothing, and other essentials.

Certainly the sixty miles so far had been a long, often discouraging plod, but there had been lighter moments as well: The "razz-ma-tazz" which had become Helen's stock answer for anything requiring a sarcastic reply; Helen's maintaining her toilet privacy by the use of a poncho; her patient listening to the innumberable quips concerning her apparent pessimistic expectation of rain at the damnedest times; and our gags about Jon putting sleeping pills in Ralph's stew, so he could be "alone" with Helen at night.

Someone suggested that instead of bathing, since we were going to throw the soap away when the water became scarce, we simply swap underwear once a week. We solemnly offered up the food we couldn't eat each day to the Snow Gods to assure us of good weather.

Finally finished with my reverie, I got up and circled the tents slowly, looking them over. Suddenly I was attracted by a movement high overhead. Gazing skyward I saw a large solitary raven flying at about 10,000 feet. I envied his easy access to altitude, but not his loneliness. I retired to the tent.

The next morning the plane returned and dropped the rest of our supplies. As it started down the valley, there was an accompanying roar from one of the ridges, as if in anger. Tons of snow and rock came hurling down the cliff. The avalanche spent itself in a billowing cloud, with rocks and huge pieces of ice surging out of it and bouncing along the glacier. We were safely out of reach, but the mountain hurled avalanches down from the ridges about every ten minutes, bouncing echoes around the valley long after the fury had settled. As I looked up at the summit I wondered what other plans it had to forestall our assault.

I noticed Helen as she sat on the snow meticulously apply-
ing her suntan cream. A dab to her forehead, a dab to each
cheek, while brushing her blond hair out of the way. Carefully she smoothed the cream over her face, under her chin,
into her ears and nostrils. Since 75 percent of the ultraviolet
radiation at this altitude was reflected by the snow, it could
strike some rather remote spots on the body. I recalled hearing
of a climber who badly sunburned the roof of his mouth while
panting up a peak.

"Attagirl, Helen."

She answered with a smile, never missing a dab.

"Not only will we get more burning rays up high," I explained, perhaps unnecessarily, "but the ultraviolet increases
about 15 percent per kilometer. You'll love it up there."

This time she answered with a nod, but still didn't miss a
dab.

No need to tell her that ultraviolet ages the skin, I thought.
She was developing a nice tan, though. I recalled reading
somewhere that the thickening of the outer layer of the skin
from the ultraviolet radiation afforded more protection than
the tanning. We'd all be pretty thick-skinned by the end of
this climb.

I had been complaining that my pack felt like "a gorilla on
my shoulders with spurs." During one of our breaks, Ron
caught our attention with a startling announcement.

"I've got it! I've got it!" he shouted enthusiastically. "I've
discovered a new adjustment on the pack which makes it in-
finitely easier to carry."

We gathered around him, eager to take advantage of his
newly-found wisdom.

"What is it, Ron?" several of us asked almost simultaneously.

"You open this drawstring on top, and then wear the pack
upside down."

With the air drops we had also received the problems of
salvaging and repacking broken supplies. And we had been

burdened with more fuel and food than could be carried in a single trip. Progress was now made by covering the route five times. First we would scout the route without packs, sometimes spending hours winding our way out over the glaciers, only to find our advance blocked by an impassable crevasse. I often thought that from the air we must look like a string of rats trying to find their way through a puzzle maze. Upon negotiating a reasonable distance, we would return over the route and pick up a load. Traversing the route a third time, we would deposit the load, and return for the final load. I began to look forward to the sixth trip which would carry us off the mountain.

Ralph was now putting in the route with Helen at the end of his rope. I was in the lead of my rope. We stopped for a few minutes of standing rest. I covered the few dozen yards between ropes and moved up to Helen to talk. We stood on the edge of a huge crevasse.

"Think we'll ever see the summit?" I queried.

"I've never had a doubt," she answered.

As we moved on, I came to a spot where the view of the trail behind revealed that we had been standing together on a rather flimsy-looking overhang. "My God, Ron," I shouted behind me, "look where we were standing." He gave the area a considered look, and replied, "Just goes to show, when you're talking to a woman you never know where you stand."

The days passed—laboriously we had moved our equipment and ourselves up to nine thousand feet. It was the eleventh day out of civilization and the weather was crisp. Today I was the last man in our team. The crevasse was like a hundred others. I approached as close to it as possible and cautiously placed my left foot in the footstep everyone had already used on the fragile snowbridge. But as I shifted my weight for the step across, the snow bridge disentegrated. As my plunge began, I severely arched my back. My pack crunched into the snow on the edge of the crevasse, leaving me teetering in a brace position with my legs dangling into the beckoning chasm.

"Are you going in any farther?" Kenn shouted.

He had gone into a self-arrest with his ice axe and was ready if I toppled off the edge.

"It's not among my plans," I responded, squirming backward and securing myself. After a few seconds' rest I reapproached the crevasse, found a more suitable crossing spot, and followed the team. We had won another skirmish in the battle.

With the passing of time and the increasing severity of the weather, we had become greatly skilled in conducting bowel functions in record time. However, we realized that in gaining this necessary proficiency we had lost the classical time for meditation. From that point we deduced that this was undoubtedly the reason the Eskimo had made such a meager contribution to culture.

Evening arrived and Ron agreed to do the cooking. With a look of great inspiration he began shredding cheese, mixing in tuna fish, and adding other odds and ends. He placed the cooking pan over the stove. As the minutes pased, fumes began evolving from the gooey mass, filling the tent with a most noxious odor. He looked up, his eyes tearing, but with a smile of accomplishment and announced that his tuna-cheese fondue was ready.

"Don't you think you ought to offer some to the other tent first?" Kenn asked.

"Right," said Ron.

He thrust the steaming pot out the opening of our tent into the opening of the other tent. Jon received it and took it inside.

It took about thirty seconds before Jon pushed the pot back into our tent, with the cautious comment, "Er . . . Ron . . . most of us in here don't want any, but thanks."

Ron took the pot and with fire in his voice announced, "If you gentlemen don't eat this, and we have to toss it to the Snow Gods, you're going to see four days of the worst weather in history."

As I shoveled a portion into my bowl, I was hoping against hope that it didn't taste like it looked and smelled. I was never quite sure if Ron had given vent to his artistic impulses or his hostility. It was unbearable.

The next day found our party moving steadily along the glacier. The going was tedious but technically easy. We were approaching the ten thousand foot level and the weather was clear except for a small cloud drooped over the ridge ahead. I was perspiring profusely, clothed only in wool pants, T-shirt, and my wind parka. As I plodded along with pack and snow-shoes, the heat seemed to increase. My goggles were continually fogging and sweat dripped from the rims. Suddenly a refreshingly cool breeze struck me. But the first few seconds of exhilaration were rapidly replaced by a wave of shivering cold. The small cloud on the ridge ahead was rolling down the mountain like a giant snowball, becoming larger and darker as it gathered speed. Minutes before we had been drenched with enormous heat and sweat, now we were about to be battered by a dark snow impregnated wind. The mountain had changed its mood. There was no point in trying to climb in these conditions. Progress had to be halted. We shoveled a level area and pitched our tents.

As I lay in my sleeping bag and listened to the howling wind, I thought of the past ten days on the mountain: avalanches crashing down and being swallowed by the gaping glaciers; the rumbling lurch of the glacial movement; the burning pain of eating salt through cracked and bleeding lips; dried, weathered, hard skin; living dirty inside heavy clothing and body odor; rubbing the food crumbs from our beards to prevent molding; never a flower, never a tree, never an animal, never a stream, not even a puddle; probing a safe campsite, erecting the tents, striking the tents, again and again; leaving a trail that twisted, sometimes backtracked, hopped over some crevasses, disappeared into others, wound gradually upward over tons of broken, distorted masses of moving ice and snow. An avalanche of sleep tumbled softly over me.

4 ▲
Karsten's Ridge

TAKE FIVE MEN and one woman, bend their spirits with fifty miles of backpacking through wilderness made up of icy rivers charged with rapids, mosquito-infested marshes, and snow fields. Make the snow deep, so that snowshoes are required most of the time. Plan their route across glaciers of enormous, shifting, broken crevasses and drop some of them into them occasionally. Scorch them with the sun, freeze them with the cold, batter them with the wind, and hurl avalanches at them. Then, add a time factor—say about ten days. Make them sleep on snow and secure all their water by melting snow for the last six of the ten days.

Now take this somewhat battered little group, place them at the ten thousand foot level on the highest peak on the North American continent, and face them with an almost vertical snow ridge rising a thousand feet from the glacier on one end and almost five thousand feet on the other. As an added morale builder, name the two peaks on the north end after two climbers killed in 1932 and the steep slope on the south end after a guide killed in 1947. From this point our climb of Karsten's Ridge begins.

We had done little more than probe out a safe campsite amid the crevasses when the silence was shattered with a thunderous roar. An immense piece of Harper's Glacier next to the upper end of the ridge had broken loose. Dropping almost four thousand feet, it crashed into the valley with an explosive boom. A huge cloud of fine snow and ice mushroomed thousands of feet into the air and rolled toward us. We braced our backs against it, and shielded our mouths to prevent inhalation of the ice crystal cloud. The icy breath blew past us and disappeared into the valley. We proceeded to establish camp.

The next morning I was sitting by the tent with a plastic bowl of hot cereal cupped in my hands. The warmth felt extraordinarily good. I was gazing at the ridge. Snow was being whipped upward along its edge, streaming a hundred feet into the air, giving it a smoking appearance. I wondered just how bad the winds would be. Up to a speed of seventy miles per hour, wind greatly increases the loss of body heat. Above that speed there is little further effect, but I couldn't get much reassurance from that thought. My reverie was jarred by Kenn's voice.

"Gene, Ron, let's rope up and give it a go. Jon, Helen, and Ralph can move a load of equipment up to the base of the ridge."

I drank the rest of my cereal and gripped the empty bowl for a few seconds, trying to drain out the last bit of heat. The frozen coils of rope handled like cable; I secured myself into the center of the rope with a bowline knot, laboriously strapped on my snowshoes, and picked up my ice axe. Kenn had moved about sixty feet toward the base of the ridge and the rope was becoming taut, so I moved out, trailing rope to Ron.

At the foot of the ridge we stashed our snowshoes. The going would be too steep for them, and we should reach wind-packed snow before long. Our assault was begun by Kenn working himself up a twisted ice chute leading to a small, patio-sized snow plateau. Under Kenn's belay I cautiously followed his route. I then brought Ron up in the same manner. We were now about a hundred feet above the surface of the glacier. We sat, resting for several minutes, and surveyed the possible route ahead. Kenn and I then anchored ourselves with our ice axes, and Ron started up the steep snow wall, shoveling and cutting steps.

He was about fifty feet above me when a rough ripping sound occurred; simultaneously I felt myself drop three or four inches. We were frozen in our tracks. I was terrified. A horizontal crack had developed just above Ron. We were standing on a slab avalanche. Would it continue downward or just hang there? A full thirty seconds elapsed before we even talked.

"Shall I proceed?" shouted Ron.

"I think so," responded Kenn. "I think it might hang up on this little plateau. What do you think, Gene?"

"I think we ought to try some other spot on the ridge. I don't like it." A wave of apprehension was still clinging to me.

"Try it a little farther, Ron," Kenn shouted. "See if you can tell how deep the crack goes."

The shoveling began again. Small pieces of snow tumbled down from his labor, like miniature avalanches. A few minutes later Ron answered Kenn's question. "It's deeper than our steps. We'd go with it if it goes."

About thirty minutes later Ron stopped. "Don't like the looks of it, Kenn. It's becoming lots steeper and it's still thigh-deep powder."

Kenn looked up at the ridge, dropped his gaze, set his jaw, and shook his head several times. "O.K., come on down."

Sometime later we had moved down the chute, and were back on the glacier where we had begun. Jon, Ralph, and Helen had moved a load of supplies up to this point, hoping the route would go. We put our snowshoes back on, and proceeded farther up the glacier, paralleling the ridge.

About two hundred yards farther we again found an area worth attacking. Again we stashed our snowshoes. This time we began working our way up an oblique ledge of snow-covered ice, broken at intervals by crevasses. The hours passed —belaying, chopping steps, jumping crevasses, shoveling, gasping with fatigue. The icy winds howled into our parkas while the heat of strenuous physical exertion poured out. Finally, the tip of the ridge was almost ours. As we approached, we were met by a blast of snow-laden wind. Before looking into the valley below, I belayed Kenn up, just as Ron had done for me. I looked about me. A feeling of intense awe came over me.

We were standing on a wide spot on the ridge—just wide enough for the three of us. In every direction mammoth silent snow sentinels rose from a base of fluffy clouds and climbed to an unbelievable ruggedness, most of them unnamed and unclimbed. Directly in front of me, to the east, was a thousand foot drop to the Traleika Glacier. It was like some ancient cracked road disappearing down a valley. Behind me was a thousand foot drop to the Muldrow Glacier, offering a similar appearance. I looked for dark dots that might be Jon, Helen, or Ralph, but clouds were beginning to fill the valley. To the north the ridge rose to Mount Koven and Mount Carpé, monuments to lost climbers. To the south, like a white sheet draped over a clothesline, the ridge climbed to a rocky prominence known as Browne's Tower, located at fifteen thousand feet. A feeling of triumph swept me as I absorbed the magnificence. However, this was quickly blown away by a chilling flurry of snow against my bearded face. All the valleys were now filling with clouds; wind and snow was beginning to batter us, obstructing our vision.

"Better dig in for a while," shouted Kenn.

In a few minutes we had scooped a notch out of the ridge. We sat with our backs against the snow bank, arms crossed and heads pulled into our parkas. The wind howled over our heads, and gradually several inches of drifted snow covered us. Our dark faces peered out of the snow like three animals looking out of their holes.

Perhaps an hour passed before I realized I had been falling asleep. I awoke with a start. Ron's eyes were closed, Kenn slept serenely. The howling wind seemed to be the only alert member of our party, and it gave no indication of relaxing its vigil. Many a mountaineer has been lulled to sleep and to doom by missing an opportunity to escape before all routes are closed by worsening conditions.

"Ron, come on, let's go." I gave him a light kick with my boot. The snow cracked around him as he moved.

"Kenn, wake up." I shoved him with my elbow. "This storm may last a week. It's time to get off this ridge." He shook himself a little and squinted over at me.

"I guess you're right," he responded.

Ron got up and brushed off the snow. He took a couple of steps and then sat down again. "We're going to need our crampons," he shouted. "It's icing up."

We began strapping our crampons to our feet. Kenn was mumbling disgustedly. "What's wrong, Kenn?" I asked.

"The laces are too short. I meant to fix them before I left, but I forgot. I'll have to go down without them."

"O.K., you go first, we'll keep the rope tight. If you slip, we'll have you."

Kenn started off the ridge, traveling very slowly. Every few feet he stopped. Finally, after about fifty feet, he turned and started back up. I took in rope to avoid slack. He approached us like a blind man, thumping the snow ahead of him with his ice axe. His goggles were completely opaque with ice. He raised them to reveal his glasses in a similar state.

"I'll have to go behind," his voice was quickly carried of by the wind. "I can't see our trail, and it's almost completely covered by snow."

Ron took the lead. Slowly we wound down the icy slopes. The wind and snow whipped at us, freezing our beards to our goggles and edges of clothing, covering our faces with heavy masks of ice.

The last of the ridge was finally dissolved by our descent, and wearily we entered camp. But our fatigue was happily lightened by our success in finding a route up the ridge.

I was awakened by the biting crispness of the air and the soft glow of sunlight in our tent. It was morning. Attired in both clothes and sleeping bag, I clumsily crawled to the tent flap and peered out. The sky was clear. The mountain looked almost inviting. The ridge had to be traveled while the weather was with us.

"It's a perfect day," I exclaimed. Kenn and Ron crawled over for a look.

"Hey! let's go," Kenn shouted. A murmur of voices filtered from the other tent.

It took about an hour to dress, cook breakfast, fill our canteens with melted snow, and hoist on our packs. Ron shuffled off through the snow, trailing rope. Our loaded ascent had begun. We carefully followed the slight dimpling in the snow, all that remained of our previous day's trail. Some hours later, Kenn, Ron, and I broke out on top of the ridge—the site of our short bivouac the previous evening—and deposited our loads. We were again greeted by the glistening magnificence. We gazed toward the summit. The ridge up to Browne's Tower had been honed to a knifelike edge by wind blowing up both sides. Ron began shoveling the edge off and moving slowly upward. The shoveled fragments of snow tumbled endlessly into the valleys below us. He was thigh-deep in powder snow. As our rope team strung out, I began to worry about the snow conditions. I wondered whether the fresh snow would cling to the surface underneath or would shear away into the valley carrying several unwilling passengers.

As we progressed we were frequently engulfed in small snow flurries raised by the wind. We had traveled about one hundred yards when suddenly our morale was skewered by a muffled rip in the snow. I felt a film of perspiration burn out onto my skin as I froze in my tracks.

A crack had developed directly along the top of the ridge. There was no way of knowing if it would avalanche to the right or to the left. Ron slowly turned his head and shoulders toward me without changing his footing. I nodded my awareness. We had already discussed the only available strategy. If Ron began to slide or tumble down one side, I would dive off the cliff to the other. Kenn would alternate with me. We would attempt to hang our rope up over the ridge in this manner. Ron pressed onward. About seventy-five yards later another warning rip chilled us. Ron moved up to a wider spot and signaled the need for a conference. None of us relished the idea of bunching our weight on the ridge, but we had to make a decision—should we proceed or abandon our hope of ascent? We were already behind schedule. To fail on Karsten's Ridge meant complete failure. We would have to leave the mountain.

As I approached Ron, I could see that his eyes were dark with apprehension. He looked extremely tired and older than his twenty-six years. As we gathered, he spoke.

"As far as I'm concerned, we've had it. Why we haven't tumbled into the valley yet, I don't know, but we can't continue on luck alone."

"What do you think, Kenn?" I asked. Several seconds elapsed before he answered.

"I suppose Ron is right," he answered. "Slab avalanches often are a half-mile long. I don't understand why one hasn't continued on down."

Ron spoke again. "I wouldn't think of climbing under these conditions in Washington, and I don't understand why we should do it now."

"I can answer that," I interjected. "I don't think we can expect the problems in expedition mountaineering to be the same as those in our own backyard. I expected to encounter problems that would strain our skill."

"But this—" Ron interrupted. "I find that I'm spending most of the time thinking of my wife and daughter, and that's no way to climb a mountain."

I looked over at Jon. He looked especially lean and hard with his ruddy face and reddish beard. I realized that Ron, in leading, had been subjected to the full impact of the cracking ridge. Jon, Helen, and Ralph had not experienced the ripping drop. Although they had followed us, the route had been tested and passed by our rope team.

"What do you think, Jon?" I asked.

He squinted up the ridge. "I think we ought to continue upward," he answered. Ralph agreed with him. Helen was undecided.

"Ron," I began, "we've had three of these slabs start with us, and each time they've stopped. I think maybe they won't break loose with us."

"How long do you expect our luck to last?" he asked by way of answering.

I gazed around the surrounding ridges. "I don't see any other avalanche activity. Perhaps it's not as bad as we think." I knew I was groping for reasons.

"Nobody's walking on those ridges," he answered.

I didn't like being the sole spokesman for continuing the ascent, especially with the mixed emotions that were clouding my judgment. "Kenn, you're our climb leader. If you say we ought to go home, I agree. No further questions, no hard feelings, that's it." The rest of our team immediately agreed.

We awaited Kenn's decision. He looked into the valleys, along the ridges, and toward the summit. "That's a decision I won't make," he finally said. "This trip means too much to all of us for me to decide. We'll have to settle it some other way."

A hush fell over our small group. Only the wind continued its murmur.

"Let's take a vote," I suggested, sounding ridiculous even to myself for suggesting such an unorthodox method of solving a climbing problem.

Helen had been quiet up to this point. "I won't vote," she said.

"Why not?" I asked.

"Well, it's different with me. I want to do what the rest of you decide. I'll count the votes."

I didn't want to argue with her. Already I was afraid I had argued too vehemently for continuing the assault, and I was neither sure nor fond of my stand. The idea of voting was not received with much enthusiasm. We had already spent over an hour in discussion.

"Tell you what," I began, "we'll close our eyes and take a vote by raising our hands, Helen will count the votes, and only she will know who votes how. We'll follow the results without ever a complaint, agreed?"

The idea was accepted. We closed our eyes. I wondered if I'd laugh in future years about this. The vote was taken.

"Which way, Helen?" several of us asked almost simultaneously.

"Up," she answered. "The vote was three to go up, two to go down."

I looked toward Ron. He was stirring aimlessly at the snow with his ice axe.

We began our trip back to camp, in order to move the last of our gear onto the ridge. I felt a certain relief in having reached a decision, right or wrong.

Ron was a changed man. He would answer quietly when spoken to but didn't initiate conversations. There was neither bitterness nor contentment; he appeared devoid of emotion. His keen sense of humor was gone. His spirit had been washed away. He was suffering from a kind of battle fatigue, and the rest of us were in pretty much the same condition. I didn't know of any cure.

We left camp late the following day, but when we did, a kind of transformation had taken place. We had come to peace with ourselves. Ron's humor had returned. We were ready to accept our fate, as tragic as it might be. We began climbing, almost ignoring our peril.

It took us several hours to reach our previous altitude. We continued upward with Jon in the lead. Suddenly a hundred-foot-long crack developed, heralded by a sound like a giant puff of wind. As we plodded onward the crack gradually opened—a quarter inch, a half inch. If it went, Jon would slide to the left. I readied myself to plunge to the right. An inch—a sense of relief swept me as I stepped widely over the end of the crack. I looked back at our second rope team, anxiously watching their progress. In a few minutes they joined us on the snow platform from which we had watched. We looked up the glistening ice wall before us. The snow was becoming harder and more windswept, the greatest danger of slab avalanche was behind us. Another victory had been eked out. Our spirits were improving.

Kenn started working up the ice cliff, the sound of his metallic chopping briskly stabbing at the air, ice chips tinkling down the wall. When he reached the top he drove a snow picket into the surface and fastened a fixed rope to it. One by one we began following his route, steadying ourselves on the rope. We rested a few moments, and Jon took the lead again.

We advanced along the ridge, shoveling, placing fixed ropes where needed, finally coming upon a four-hundred-foot-long area of ridge that had been wind-whipped to a knife edge and frozen in position. Jon surveyed it apprehensively. He turned and looked toward me. I was motionless. Clouds drifted in the two-thousand-foot void on either side. At the end was the only wide spot in the entire ridge—our campsite if we could conquer it. Gripping the head of his ice axe in both hands, Jon drove it vertically into the knife edge ahead of him. He then advanced his feet on either side, cautiously withdrew his axe, and again drove it in front of him. Slowly he began to advance. I belayed him until the rope was played out, and then began to follow in a similar fashion. I almost laughed at the absurd precariousness of our position. When he reached the wide area, he belayed me the rest of the way across.

We dropped exhaustedly into the soft snow and sat for some time. We had the feeling that we were slowly winning the battle. We unloaded our packs and headed down for another load.

It was late evening before we arrived back. Our campsite at 12,500 feet measured about one hundred by two hundred feet. We could walk about with minimum danger. The shackles of the ridge had been released for a while.

Our spirits were beginning to soar. Another twenty-five hundred feet would conquer the ridge. We looked up the formidable icy pitch to Browne's Tower. Kenn began to sing, "Mr. Browne, Mr. Browne, here we come."

After supper we sat watching the sun that had just settled into the northern sky. It hung there on the horizon, as if resting before continuing its daily circle. In a few hours it would rise from the north, circle the sky, and return again to settle in the north. There was no darkness during this time of the year, but a sort of melancholy dusk blanketed the land. A lingering pink was reflected from the white mountain tops, and I realized I was watching a magnificent sunset-sunrise that would last all "night." We talked briefly about when it ceased to be dusk and began to be dawn, but no one could answer the question. We quietly retired to our tents.

Suddenly all was whiteness, I was falling, being buried under tons of snow. I flailed my arms . . . I awoke with a start. I looked up at the white inner-tent wall. Kenn and Ron slept peacefully. I looked at my watch—5 a.m. The air was crisp, my face was very cold. I pulled down into my sleeping bag, and sleep again soaked into me.

After breakfast we sat around in the snow preparing our equipment for the next phase of our battle. Our spirits were subdued compared to the previous night. We wanted to be certain that our assault tools were in top shape. I took the file from our repair kit and began to hone my crampons to a fine point. These were the steel toes I would need to claw up the mountain. Next I began sharpening my ice axe. I rolled the shaft over in my hand inspecting the glistening steel ends. It's quite a weapon I thought, recalling the times it had saved my life by impaling a mountain that was attempting to dash me to infinity. I thrust it into the snow and twisted it. A creaky squeak responded as if in protest. I felt like a medieval soldier preparing for combat.

Having completed the preparations, I sat looking at my companions. We were on the verge of a new problem. I looked into each face, wondering how each of us would tolerate the effects of high altitude. It was going to get much colder. For every thousand feet of altitude the temperature decreases about three-and-a-half degrees Fahrenheit. We would lose more heat through the necessity of deep breathing, and the increased wind would rob us of still more. However, I felt that we were well equipped to tolerate cold. But certain of the effects would be unavoidable, like the dehydration. We would lose enormous amounts of fluid through breathing and evaporation—more than twice what a person loses at sea level—and our problems of replacement depending entirely on the melting of snow would be overwhelming. We would need something like four to seven quarts of water per man per day to avoid dehydration. That's forty-two quarts or ten-and-a-half gallons a day for our party.

Even at fourteen thousand feet the lowered barometric pressure allowed an arterial oxygen pressure of only 50 percent of that at sea level, and at twenty thousand feet it dropped to about one third of the sea level value. We were bound to have our problems—the headaches, breathlessness, nausea, loss of appetite, dry cough, sleeplessness, and lassitude. How well would we tolerate them? I felt despair. Despair not just for these unavoidable companions of altitude, but especially for the really serious threats—the severe losses of judgment, the confusion, hallucinations, and even coma.

The assault was again under way, and my mind was kept busy with keeping the rope taut, swinging it from right to left on the switchbacks, frequently checking the knots, dodging the pieces of ice falling from the step-cutting above me, gripping the ice axe with a clawlike grip, and every once in a while the brief standing rests, like oases.

We were crossing the area of Thayer's Fall now. It was a

four thousand foot drop to the glacier below—a rather sobering thought, but not one to think about while climbing. I wondered if the name would be changed after I also fell there.

The slope was too steep and icy to allow an arrest with an ice axe. Any slip would mean almost certain death to our entire rope team. Occasionally my balance would waver for a split second as my pack shifted, and I would be momentarily wracked by an indescribable fear. I recalled that the fear of falling is one of the few basic unlearned fears inherent in man.

Catching a crampon point in my rope, bootlace, or wind-pants; a tug on the rope from a team member; a sharp gust of wind; a piece of a falling snow mass dislocated from above—any of these things could certainly cause me to stumble. Each foot, each stroke of the ice axe was placed with precise deliberation. I realized that each next step might be the biggest and also the most important step in my life. I was already developing an intense dread for the trip down to secure the second load, and the repetition of this part of our ascent.

Gradually the ridge began to level as we approached within a hundred yards of Browne's Tower. As we climbed, the summit of Mount McKinley came into view, its huge ice dome boldly crowning the North American continent.

"There it is!" Kenn shouted.

No one answered.

We stared through squinted eyes as the sun illuminated the massive top. We were all flooded with the exhaltation that victory would be ours; only a few more days of dogged pushing would see us on the summit. My mind ran briefly over the difficulties we had encountered thus far but they were submerged by another look toward the snowy crown.

As I trod methodically onward, breathing forty times per minute and taking only one step every three seconds, I became acutely aware of a pain in my left shoulder. It became more intense and began radiating down my left arm. I stopped for several seconds, gasping huge breaths of the thin air. The pain disappeared. I started climbing again, and again the pain began. Was this a coronary pain? A slight shudder passed over me. We had climbed the last eight-and-a-quarter hours without a single stop for water or pack removal. Had we pushed ourselves beyond our physical capacities? At a slowed pace I painfully continued the last yards, reaching the base of Browne's Tower and dropping in a panting heap with the rest of our party.

I looked up the Harper's Glacier toward the summit. The route was covered with deep powder snow. Our hopes for an easy trip on hard, wind-packed snow were dashed. The going would be laborious, but neither dangerous nor technically difficult. A feeling of hope stirred within me, and then went out. What about the pain down my arm? If I was suffering from angina at fifteen thousand feet, I certainly could go no farther, and perhaps couldn't even survive the trip out.

I looked over at Kenn. He was grimacing and rubbing his left shoulder.

"Something wrong, Kenn?"

He took several deep breaths before he answered, "I don't know. I developed a pain down my left arm during this last pitch."

I wondered, could we both be suffering from angina? We had undergone the same stresses, and at thirty-three years of age, we were in the age bracket where coronary occlusion can occur. I was annoyed at the irony of the situation—to surpass so many obstacles, and finally to become a casualty in this manner.

Our plan had been to return to 12,500 feet for the night, and in the morning move our camp up to this point. The following day would be spent moving our camp to 16,500. From that point we could make a summit bid, or move our camp to one further location. I thought it time for a council.

"Kenn, I developed the same type of pain. It's suggestive of the pain of coronary insufficiency. I'll give it to you straight. If our hearts are starving for blood, we'll be lucky to get off this mountain without precipitating a heart attack."

Kenn and the others sat quietly.

"However," I continued, explaining as if I were talking to one of my patients, "there is the possibility that this is pain from ischemic shoulder muscle—that is, pain originating in the shoulder from lack of sufficient blood oxygen. This could also extend down the arm."

"Why don't we have it in our leg muscles, then?" Kenn asked. "They're working harder than anything else."

I squinted my eyes for a few seconds, collecting my thoughts. "In doing a rest step we pause after each step, allowing the muscles to become renourished, but our packs hang on our shoulders continuously." The logic seemed sound.

"How can we tell if it's heart or just shoulder?" Ron asked.

"With a kind of exercise tolerance test," I answered. "Kenn can exercise without his pack, if the pain occurs, then it's heart. If he only becomes exhausted we're safe." I directed Kenn to exercise, with the warning to stop immediately if pain occurred.

Kenn began hopping around us, jumping occasionally on one foot, stopping for a couple of deep knee bends, occasionally waving an arm. It was a kind of bizarre dance that grew slower and slower, as Kenn's lips grew bluer. Within thirty seconds he gulped at the air, and flew back in sitting position, chest heaving and eyelids trying to clear the tears glazing his eyes. We crowded around him.

"Does it hurt, Kenn?" I asked. He continued to puff and gasp, too breathless to talk.

"Kenn, does it hurt?" I repeated, with anxiety in my voice. He stared straight ahead, blinking, panting. He bent his head forward slightly, swallowed, and slowly lifted his head toward our tense faces. A faint smile broke across his face as he gasped, "No."

5 ▲
A Near Disaster

It wasn't a sound sleep. You couldn't afford the luxury of a sound sleep anymore. A kind of pilot light was kept burning, ready to spring into action if an emergency arose. Frequently a soft tumbling occurred against my sleeping bag as Kenn and Ron restlessly slept in their state of suspended anxiety. It was darker than it should have been, and the wind was beginning to whip the tent unmercifully. The staccato slaps, and the variable pitch whining caused me to sink a little deeper into the security of my sleeping bag. A mist of fine ice crystals surrounded the small opening in the top of the bag where my breath had frozen onto the material. I was becoming aware of the fine crisp pummeling of snow against the tent, when I felt Ron rise to a sitting position in his bag. There were a few seconds of considered analysis, and then with a resigned sigh he said, "We've got to start shoveling. Our tent is being buried." I also rose to a sitting position. I squinted my eyes and brought up my wrist—2 a.m.

The weight of the snow caving in the sides had shrunk the small interior of our tent to a still smaller size. Ron struggled out of his bag into the biting crispness of the air and began crawling into his down clothing, panting and sometimes gasping as he physically engaged himself against the thin air and stiff frozen clothing. Finally, he disappeared out the tent opening into a swirling dark abyss. His shoveling sounded lost and very distant amid the howling and flapping that surrounded us. His faint scraping continued for perhaps twenty minutes.

During the day Ralph and I had put in a route and carried

a load of supplies nearly a thousand feet up the glacier. Kenn, Ron, and Helen had agreed to break camp and join us. They had never shown up, being reluctant to break camp with impending bad weather. We had trudged back down, leaving a cache of supplies. I wondered if we would be able to find them after this storm.

With a burst of icy wind and snow, Ron lunged into the tent and zipped the flapping door. He turned slowly toward us. It was quiet, and he looked like a lifeless statue covered with frost. The rim of hair protruding along the edge of his parka was frozen to it. His beard was a mass of hard ice, with a pile up on his lip where his running nose had frozen into his mustache. His face was blanched and his eyes, peering from within the ring of frosted eyelashes, appeared deep, dark, and frightened. Slowly he spoke, his speech slurred through the chapped lips and mound of ice around his mouth. "We may be in trouble. I don't know how we'll be able to keep up with the shoveling. I couldn't finish . . ." The tent flapping in the whining wind drowned out the last of his words.

"I'll go out next," I said with a mixture of duty and apprehension.

I laboriously pulled on my clothing, stopping every few seconds to rest, and breathing as rapidly as I could. Equipped with enormous insulated rubber boots and bulky down clothing, I moved somewhat stiff-armed, as if I had been overinflated. I pulled a chamois skin face mask perforated only by narrow eye slits and nostril holes over my head, and crawled into the swirling, howling whiteness.

I had expected intense cold and violent wind, but I suddenly became aware that my expectations were meager compared to what I was experiencing. You can't anticipate a violence you've never known. As I pulled the short-handled aluminum shovel out of the tent, the wind snatched it from me and sailed it erratically over my head at the end of my nylon wrist cord. I yanked it down and gripped it firmly. The wind blast against my face mask made breathing difficult. I took a step in the powdery, thigh-deep snow—a somewhat off-balance step. The wind took immediate advantage, delivering a gusty punch which sprawled me into the snow. I crawled to my feet, and carefully planting each step, leaning far into the wind, using the shovel as support, I moved slowly around the tent.

Crouched with my back against the wind, I turned my head and glanced toward the summit. Within a second or two my tearing eyelids were frozen together. Suddenly blinded, I removed my right hand from the elbow-length mitten and ran my hand up under my face mask to melt my frozen lids. In these few seconds my finger tips began screaming with icy pain. I quickly thrust my hand back into my mitten, only to find it half-full of wind driven snow.

I huddled down in the snow, planning my next move. All my time so far had been spent fighting the storm. I hadn't even begun to shovel off the tent. In a mood of frustrated anger I got up and began vigorously shoveling. As the shovelful was lifted a couple inches, the wind scattered the contents, almost instantly filling the defect with more snow. I worked faster and harder. The wind howled its whistling mockery into the edges of my parka. I was totally ineffectual.

A dark moving mass became apparent about fifteen feet from me. I recognized it as Jon attempting to dig out our other mountain tent. One of the tent cords had been ripped from the side, leaving a fluttering hole. A fiberglass support rod was broken, sticking out through the tent like a broken bone. One of the aluminum tent posts was badly bent.

We moved toward one another until our grizzly faces were scant inches apart. We grasped each other's shoulders to brace ourselves against the turbulent fury. "Better get food inside," shouted Jon, "packs almost buried." I nodded.

We moved slowly toward our packs. The previous evening our packs had stood three feet out of the snow, propped against our ice axes. Now only the tops of two packs peered from beneath the snow. The other four were already buried.

Jon wrestled one free from the snow, and pulled a large plastic food bag out of the top. I took it from him and together we unzipped the flapping tent door and thrust the package inside. I almost dove after it, carrying a bit of the storm with me into the tent. After securing the tent door I turned toward Ron and Kenn. The interior of the tent seemed amazingly comfortable. I pulled off my frozen boardlike face mask.

Kenn spoke first. "How is it?"

"Rougher than I've ever seen it," I replied. "I couldn't accomplish a thing."

"How are Jon, Helen, and Ralph making out?"

"Worse than we are. Their tent is torn and bent. Jon was shoveling; Helen and Ralph were inside trying to keep things together."

Kenn began putting on his arctic gear. I stripped off some of my heavy frozen outer garments and stacked them near the door. In a few minutes Kenn was ready. As he disappeared through the door, the storm probed an icy finger into the tent.

Ron and I sat waiting and thinking. Little conversation passed between us. Finally Kenn crawled back into the tent, vigorously brushing off the clinging snow. His glasses were etched by a layer of ice. "I can't see anything; I had to feel my way back into the tent. Jon, Helen, and Ralph are losing their tent. It's past the point of saving. Pile all our gear in the end of the tent. They'll be joining us in a few minutes."

No sooner had he finished than there was a gust of wind, and the air filled with snowflakes as the tent door was opened. The end of a sleeping bag was thrust into the tent. We quickly pulled it in, beating off the snow as it came as if it had been covered with noxious insects. Two more bags followed, then a procession of three duffel bags containing personal gear. Helen, Ralph, and Jon then crawled in, piling on top of the gear and each other. We vigorously brushed the snow off them as they came, and zipped the door after them.

We were extremely crowded. A tent that had been made for two people, but which could cozily accommodate three, was now packed with six. And the encroachment of the snow on the tent had decreased its size by at least a quarter. We packed our gear into the ends of the tent and placed ourselves alternately with our feet against one wall and backs against the other. We hoped that bracing ourselves in this manner would prevent the weight of the snow from further crushing our tent. Already the tent was too small to allow us to stretch out our legs.

The hours passed. The storm continued. Our joints now ached agonizingly. More hours passed. With each shift of position the snow would gain a few more inches. No matter how hard you pushed and rammed, the lost space was irretrievable. More hours passed. The wind screamed eerily. We watched the level of the snow slowly rise outside the tent.

The outer tent wall now had a large rip in the side, and snow was being forced between the tent walls. We were now cramped with our knees almost to our chins, our necks bent with our chins on our chests, squashed against each other. I had a sudden terrifying feeling of claustrophobia. With all my will power I fought the urge to kick my legs, thrust out my arms, and claw out of this diminishing-room torture chamber.

Kenn, our climb leader, spoke. There was no hint of anxiety in his voice; in fact, he sounded rather matter-of-fact: "I don't think we can survive more than another five or six hours of this or we'll be forced to abandon whatever's left of this tent."

It wasn't necessary for him to say more. We all knew what he meant. If we were forced out into the storm, it would mean certain death.

It wasn't as if we had a chance to get off the mountain. We had just spent seventeen hazardous days, utilizing all our available skill, teamwork, and special equipment to gain this altitude of 16,350 feet. Without any one of these elements our ascent to this point would have been inconceivable. Our ropes and most of our equipment were already wind-scattered and buried. I wondered whether we would be able to find sufficient equipment to make our way off the mountain even if the storm subsided. Or would we end up as an infinitesimal speck frozen into one of the huge glaciers?

I looked at my watch—10 a.m. I had not eaten in twenty-two hours. Most of our food was dehydrated. We had no water. In fact, we had seen no naturally occurring water for almost two weeks. All our water was obtained by melting snow with our two stoves, both of which were buried somewhere outside. The thought occurred to me that we might perish through weakness from hunger and dehydration.

The tent shuddered with the wind, as if possessed by a giant chill. It didn't seem to matter much how we were going to die, but die we must. I had always thought how I would fight to prevent death but how could I fight this?

I looked around the tent. It seemed incredible and ironic that six people in perfect health would be dead within a day or two.

Kenn looked grief-stricken. As leader of our expedition he undoubtedly felt an extra responsibility. As an engineer he was desperately seeking a mechanical solution to the apparently inevitable fate. He had already attempted unsuccessfully to brace the inside of the tent with pack board frames. He had also conceived the idea of uncovering one tent, freeing it from its snow anchors, and then rolling back and forth to stay on top of the advancing snow—theoretically a good idea, but doomed by the impossibility of uncovering the base of the tent. He placed his head in his mittened hands and frowned in painful concentration.

Helen looked up. Her sun-tanned, freckled face was silhouetted by her short-cropped strawberry blond hair. Many doubts had been raised when we included her in our team, but she had proven herself an asset in almost every way. "Well, it won't be very long before we're just six little snowmen," she said with a strained half-smile. It was her way of saying that she understood the odds against us. We muttered an acknowledgement.

I looked toward Jon. He also tried a smile. It was obviously a smile of attempted reassurance. Most of it was accomplished with his clear blue eyes glistening above a light, mottled growth of reddish-brown beard. I wondered what he thought our chances of survival were.

Ralph was at the end of the tent. He sat hunched over, looking at nothing. He was unusually quiet, and his thick brown beard lent a false fullness to his thin haggard face. Ron, our youngest member, sat brooding and thinking behind his black beard. We had made many sacrifices in putting this expedition together, but Ron had exceeded us all. It had been necessary for him to quit his job; he had left his wife alone with their two-month-old firstborn; he had borrowed money and would arrive home broke and in debt if he arrived at all.

I'm not sure who first suggested the plan, but all of a sudden we were all talking about the possibility of digging an ice cave. The labor involved was staggering—pushing ourselves into the storm, chiseling, picking, and shoveling a room large enough for six people. We finally agreed that it was probably impossible to dig a room large enough for all, but perhaps a couple could survive. This seemed acceptable.

Ron and Jon were nearest the tent flap. They twisted out into the thrashing whiteness taking our two small shovels with them. Together they frantically worked to make a permanent dent in the snow slope. For every four or five shovelfuls they removed, three or four came back. Sometimes they simply clung to each other to prevent the gusts from toppling them down the mountain. Frequently they were knocked down, but digging continued. Two hours later they had created a body-sized depression. They hovered protectively over this niche, guarding it with their bodies against the fury of the wind. Their aching forms, encrusted with ice, continued their seemingly futile toil.

In the meantime Ralph and Kenn had set out to find the packs containing the stoves. They had overcome the icy hardships long enough to uncover one. This discovery was an enormous boost, since we could now eat and drink, if we could

find time. I donned my arctic gear and struggled out to bring
Ron and Jon the news of the stove. Ron was almost out of
sight. He was in the hole chopping with his ice axe; the snow
was too hard for the shovel. I crawled in behind him. Chipping
away until exhausted, he would shove the chips behind him.
I would then scoop up the chips with a cooking pot, throwing
them out the entrance way. Jon shoveled the chips and threw
them to the wind. We moaned with the cold, the fatigue, the
gnawing thirst and hunger, but we continued.

The storm seemed to be easing slightly, and our members
on the surface renewed their efforts to preserve our remaining
tent. The shovel we gave them had several broken rivets, but
if used with care it was still functional.

Twelve hours had passed since the cave had been started.
It was almost midnight. We inspected the shimmering icy
walls of our new shelter. It was about three feet high with a
diameter of six or seven feet—clearly large enough for six
squatting people. The lack of howling wind and flapping tent
lent a strange tranquility. An enormous feeling of euphoria
swept me. We could now survive, miserably perhaps, but we
could survive. As Ron chipped a few more pieces of ice from
the wall, he turned his head and smiled. It was a genuine smile.
"Isn't mountaineering fun," he said.

The cold white savagery of the storm had battered us for
twenty-four hours of tent-shredding fury and left us weary,
hungry, parched, and frostbitten, but the completion of the
ice cave had dispelled a consuming hopelessness that had been
overcoming our will to resist.

Now the intense fury of the storm was largely dissipated.
Kenn, Helen, and Ralph elected to sleep in the tent, with the
reservation that they could retreat to the ice cave if necessary.
Jon, Ron, and I stretched out on the cave floor. Sleep descended heavily upon us in our icy crypt. We were warm at
last, the wind noises were remote, and a feeling of security
possessed us. We were not aroused when the storm had swept
up the mountain during the night. Our passageway slowly

became packed full of drifting snow, but we slept on. Our ventilation hole had filled with sifting snow but we slept on. As the snow covered all traces of our cave, as the mountain began to incorporate us, like a giant carnivorous plant, we slept ever sounder, ever deeper.

Nobody knows what awakened Helen—perhaps the sun shining through the tent, perhaps the relative silence with the passing of the storm, or perhaps some unknown inner sense of apprehension and urgency. But she did awaken, hurriedly dressed, and decided to go directly to our ice cave.

The weather was beautiful—sunny, clear, and crisp—and the snow creaked under her boots as she made her way. That's strange, she thought, I must be mistaken. The cave must be over there. But it wasn't. Her steps quickened as she rapidly covered the area. But there was no evidence of a cave anywhere. She shouted, but was answered only by a murmuring of the wind.

She ran back to the tent as fast as she could negotiate the thin air and thick snow, breathlessly calling, "Ralph! Kenn!" Hurry, they're buried!"

Ralph crawled out of his sleeping bag, thinking, "Just like a woman—alarmist—can't even find the cave." Then the sharp cold and bright sun thrust him into wakefulness. He quickly confirmed Helen's discovery.

Kenn put on his boots with much grunting. He stuck his head out the door like a cautious animal, squinting into the sun, then disappeared back into the tent and crawled out with his sun goggles over his glasses.

A plan was formulated. They would systematically probe the slope beside the tent with the eight foot crevasse probing pole. The entrance to the cave would be detected by a lessened resistance to the thrust.

The air seemed saturated with cold and tension. Kenn began the probing. While thrusting, cautiously alert for the telltale soft snow, he was thinking of the hazards the team had already survived. His mind wandered some ten days back when I had effected an ice-axe arrest, which had halted his plunge between the icy, dripping crevasse walls. Maybe I can return the favor now, he thought, as he labored with the probing. Somewhat painfully he brought to mind the fury of twenty-four hours ago when, overcome with despair, he had seriously considered walking off into the storm. It seemed as if the mountain would not be appeased until it claimed part of the party. He wondered how long we had been buried. The probing continued.

Helen was possessed by an almost sickening apprehension. Jon had proposed marriage to Helen a few weeks before the expedition had begun. Now he lay somewhere underground drifting toward eternity. Her life, becoming so meaningful, now seemed to be approaching such emptiness. She wondered if we had already suffocated.

Ralph took the probing pole from Kenn and Kenn sat in the snow, panting and exhausted, his lips a thin line of blue. Ralph began the methodical task. The party had almost turned back the week before, when Ron had stated in no uncertain terms that he considered further advance on the avalanche-ridden ridge almost suicidal. Perhaps Ron had been right. He wondered if the cave would ever be found. Most of the suspect area had already been probed.

Ralph stabbed at the mountain now with vengeance, endeavoring to force the release of its prisoners. Finally his lance entered the snow with relative ease. Could this be it? He thrust again at the same spot, his breath held between clenched teeth.

A strange supernatural glow filled the cave as the sunlight filtered through the icy depths. I became sleepily aware that something was striking my foot. There it was again. This time a small shower of snow pummeled the foot of my sleeping bag, and a thin shaft of light penetrated our seclusion.

"Hello . . . hello, down there." The voice was muffled. The

probe was worked up and down several times, with more snow falling in.

"Yeah," I shouted. The air was heavy, warm, and oppressive. I could now hear a murmur of voices from the surface and the crisp sound of shoveling. Jon and Ron stirred. I picked up the shovel and began digging where our passageway had been. The surface shoveling seemed to echo my own shovel noises. All of a sudden, with a metallic clash our shovels collided. With an extended arm I cleared the last fragments of loose snow. As I finished, Ralph stuck his head into the passageway.

"You wrecked our sleep," I said with obvious irritation.

"We're glad," he said with a broad, bearded grin.

6 ▲
THE FINAL ASSAULT

DID YOU EVER go three weeks without a bath? It's surprising how your own body odor becomes more annoying than that of your companions. Did you ever spend three weeks living and sleeping on just snow? Never a tree, a river, a flower. How you miss color and the fragrance of vegetation—and music, how I missed music!

As I trudged along at eighteen thousand feet, I looked at our weary party of six climbing toward the summit of McKinley. We were now almost seventy miles from where we had first strapped on our snowshoes, and hoisted our seventy-pound packs upon our backs. In the preceding weeks we had crossed many miles of treacherous, crevassed glaciers; we had encountered incredible avalanche hazards, and had survived weather which could have easily destroyed us. It was as if we were trespassing on some alien planet.

We had spent the entire day yesterday digging out our storm-buried tents and equipment. We had left camp this morning at six, each carrying a quart of water, a can of meat, and two candy bars. We had hoped to reach the 20,320 foot summit in eight or nine hours. However, wading through miles of deep powder snow had completely destroyed our time schedule. I looked at my watch. It was almost 2 p.m., and we were only at eighteen thousand feet. As we approached Denali Pass, the snow became increasingly hard, packed by the sweeping winds.

We had reached the point where we would climb out of the glacial basin and gain altitude rapidly. We looked up the steep slope and gathered for a rest before continuing. We drank the last of our water, it was full of ice crystals. Kenn took out the thermometer and informed us of the delightful sixteen below temperature. The deep blue of the cloudless sky conveyed the impression that we were high into space. I opened a can of corned beef and began eating it. My enthusiasm for the meat was not shared by the rest of the team. As we began to chill, we reroped and resumed our climb.

We stopped at 18,300 feet to look out toward Anchorage and the complex of rivers glistening far below us with a few clouds drifting in between. The character of the snow was very different now. Mounds of snow carved by the wind stood like pieces of surrealist sculpture. Elaborate ice crystal formations hung from the rocks in fairyland fashion. The surface resembled wave action on a beach, frozen into stillness. One could have been roaming the bottom of a lifeless sea or a desert of snow. I realized how few men had ever seen these sights and how few ever would.

Our spirits were high, but fatigue and breathlessness were overtaking us. When Kenn, Ron, and I reached 18,750 feet we stopped to rest. Jon, Helen, and Ralph had lagged a considerable distance behind, and we were beginning to worry. As they approached us it was evident that they were delayed only by fatigue. They wearily dropped into sitting position, their eyes glazed with exhaustion. I uneasily realized that the last five hundred feet of altitude had effected a remarkable change. Just when I had begun to believe that the summit was within our grasp, a shadow of doubt had presented itself.

I looked at Jon's bulging pack. "What do you have in your pack, Jon?" I asked.

"The stove," he replied.

"Are we going to need it?" I inquired, turning toward Kenn.

"Probably not," Kenn answered.

Jon began removing it from his pack, working in the usual slow motion necessary at this altitude.

I looked toward the summit, only about fifteen hundred vertical feet of good snow separated us from the top of this mountain, but I could see the altitude acting like a heavy weight oppressing our drive. I took our central nervous system stimulants from my kit and we each took a tablet. After many more minutes rest, we again began our trudge. We now roped in three rope teams. I roped to Ralph and took the lead. Kenn roped to Ron, traveling almost parallel to Jon and Helen and offering them encouragement.

As I methodically plodded along, I was practically bursting with enthusiasm. The thoughts of the severe hardship and discouragement melted behind me as the summit seemed to be coming within our grasp. I looked behind and found that Ralph and I were gradually outdistancing the rest of our party.

At 19,600 feet we stood on the top edge of a valley that nestled immediately in front of the summit ridge. We had to cross the valley to approach the summit, and it meant losing several hundred feet in altitude. It was disappointing, but not devastating. The white summit dome was vividly brilliant against the clear, dark blue sky. I filled my lungs with the thin cold air and pushed onward.

We crossed the valley and started up the steep icy pitch, the last bulwark of the mountain. The going was very slow. Kenn, Ron, Helen, and Jon were getting closer now, because our progress had been slowed. We were about a hundred yards from them now, much of it vertical distance, perhaps thirty minutes ahead of them.

"Hey, Gene," Ron's voice echoed clearly through the frigid air and across the frozen surface.

I stopped and looked down. Ron was standing beside the rest of our group, looking up at us.

"Yeah," I shouted.

"Would you come down here a minute?" he asked.

I thought it was a joke.

"What for?" I shouted down.

"We need you," he responded.

A feeling of resentment stirred within me. I had so keyed myself to continue up this pitch that I was performing more like a machine than a man. It was several seconds before my altitude-numbed mind realized that he wouldn't call me down unless I was urgently needed.

I turned to Ralph and shrugged my shoulders. "Let's go," I said. We began plunge-stepping down, and had joined them within five minutes. I was shocked by what I saw.

Helen was leaning heavily against Jon; he was supporting her with his right arm. They would occasionally take a stumbling step forward. Helen looked unbelievably weary, as if she had been crying several nights without sleep. She took several rapid short breaths through bluish lips, and started to pitch backward. Ralph caught her. She opened her eyes wide and struggled to her feet again.

"She says she can't feel her feet," Ron said.

"Is that right, Helen?" I spoke directly into her face.

"I guess so," she responded between gasps.

"Helen, we have to stop," I said.

"Oh no," she almost shouted, "I've got to go on."

"But, your feet, you're developing frostbite."

"I've *got* to go on."

"Helen," I took her by the shoulders, "I know you want to climb this mountain, but is it worth losing your feet?" I thought perhaps I could shock her into reality.

"No," she answered, "but I've got to keep going." She pushed against me.

"Listen to me," I shouted, "it's not just you, we're all going to rest awhile before we proceed. We'll warm your feet while we're resting."

Her push against me had dissolved into a heavy lean.

"All right," she muttered.

"How cold is it, Kenn?" I asked. Kenn was keeper of our outdoor thermometer.

"Twenty-six degress below zero," he answered.

We moved about a hundred feet down into the valley where

the surface was level, and I began to unlace Helen's boots in order to examine her feet. I huddled over, with her feet in my lap to shield them from the wind. I pulled off her socks and hurriedly examined her toes—no visible signs except they were cold and white. Superficial frostbite, I thought to myself.

I untied the waist drawstrings on my wind parka, and thrust her feet under my clothing onto my bare abdomen. The cold was almost painful. I tucked the edges of the parka around her legs to effect a seal from the wind. The rest of our party huddled in a tight circle around her.

"She just needs warmth, water, and food," I said.

Jon opened a can of tuna fish. It was frozen completely solid. We couldn't even significantly dent the surface with a knife. Our little remaining water was frozen. The food and water problems could only be solved with a stove, which we had left at 18,750 feet.

Finally Helen's feet were almost as warm as my abdomen. Kenn produced a pair of dry wool socks which I quickly placed on her feet. Ron laid out his sleeping bag, the only one with us, and she crawled into it. She was shaking vigorously.

"Someone's going to have to go back for the stove," Kenn announced.

"I'll go." Jon's answer was immediate.

"I'll go with him," Ralph added.

"We'll see you in about four hours," Kenn said. "Good luck."

I sat down next to Helen on the windward side. Kenn sat at her feet, and Ron situated himself on her other side. I watched as Jon and Ralph slowly climbed out of the valley; in about forty-five minutes they finally disappeared.

We were shivering uncontrollably. I directed my gaze toward Helen. She seemed to be sleeping. I recalled that one of our first agreements during our initial planning of the trip was that there would be no women. Tufts of short, frost-covered blond hair framed the edge of her parka. Her freckled face looked so pale and helpless. She had been such a pillar of strength. I wondered if even now she realized her chances of reaching the summit were gone.

"Kenn," I began, "why don't you and Ron make a bid for the summit? It's only about seven hundred feet in altitude to go. Nothing further can be done for Helen anyway until Jon and Ralph return."

Ron spoke first. "Count me out. If it hadn't been Helen, it would have been me, I was just a shade behind."

Then Kenn answered, "If I had even one cup of water, I might try, but right now I don't think I could make it."

A few hours ago we were on the verge of victory and our spirits were soaring. Now we were virtually crushed. The irony was devouring me as much as the cold.

Another hour went by. I had been shivering continuously. Mostly I fought to move my progressively numbing toes. I knew I was losing the battle. The smallest toes on both feet had ceased to ache, and there was now no feeling in them. The continuous violent shaking was exhausting me, and I knew it. At the end of three hours I spent a half hour just gazing at the edge of the valley, desperately hoping for the appearance of Jon and Ralph, but they didn't appear.

"Kenn," I said, "I'm considering going to the summit by myself."

"That wouldn't be wise," he said.

I answered almost before he finished, "I know, but it's not wise to sit here and lose my toes when I could save them by climbing."

He wearily stood up and looked at the summit. It seemed very close.

"I know I've got enough energy to make it," I added. "We could climb it while Jon and Ralph are gone. When we return they can climb it. They'll have had food and water by then."

Kenn, deep in thought, didn't answer at first. "All right," he finally said, "I'll go with you."

I looked at Helen. She was dozing, apparently comfortable in the sleeping bag. We roped up and spread the rope out between us. At that moment Jon and Ralph were silhouetted against the pale gray sky. Even though they were about thirty minutes away, we decided to wait for the food and water that would be made available when the stove arrived. We agreed that this had been the most miserable bivouac we had ever spent, and we could now talk of how good the water would taste.

Finally they arrived. The stove was immediately set up, primed with alcohol, and the match struck. The flame burned with an uneven glow almost devoid of heat. We couldn't get the burner hot enough to vaporize the kerosene fuel. We tried again and again. We built a windbreaker out of ice blocks. We used every trick we knew, but to no avail. Our efforts wasted, we were right where we had started four bitter hours ago.

The mountain had dealt its last crushing blow. We looked toward the summit, but it was no longer visible. The weather was closing in and it looked like a storm was brewing. We knew we couldn't survive a storm at that altitude without equipment. I looked at my watch. It was almost 6 a.m. We had gone twenty-four hours without sleep and with little food and water.

It was Kenn that spoke. "Let's go. We've been beaten. We can't chance the weather any longer."

"Gene, we can make it." It was Ralph; he refused to give up.

"Ralph," I answered, "there's only one thing in this world that I'd rather do than climb this mountain, and that's to see home again someday. Right now I don't think the two are possible. If the weather were clear I'd go, but if we get caught in a storm, we're dead."

"Maybe it won't storm," he answered.

"It looks too bad," I countered. "I'm sorry Ralph."

Kenn and Ron led off. Helen and then Jon followed. I fell in line next with Ralph behind me.

We moved slowly across the floor of the valley, but instead of feeling crushed, I became filled with an enormous bitter hate. I had had enough of being blown, frozen, dropped, pummeled, starved, and thirsted. To get so close and be cheated out of victory was almost more than I could tolerate.

"Gene, look!" Ralph shouted.

I turned to see the summit now partly visible. Apparently a small cloud had been hanging around the summit.

"Jon," I shouted ahead, "we'll be a couple hours behind you. We're going to make a try for the summit."

I knew I was lying when I said a couple hours. He shouted something to Ron and Kenn.

"O.K.," he yelled.

An incredible flame of enthusiasm possessed me. Ralph and I fairly ran over the level hundred yards to the beginning of the summit ridge. Fatigue quickly overtook us and, panting wildly, we began a slow ascent.

We had ascended a couple hundred feet when my confidence began to stagger. Clouds were again covering the summit, and the weather looked threatening at best. I began to wonder if this wasn't the ultimate in poor judgment. I stopped and shouted down to Ralph.

"It's not too late. We can still turn back and join the others." I was looking for the slightest excuse to turn back, but Ralph wouldn't provide it.

"We can make it. Keep going," he shouted back.

I continued upward. As I began to search routes over and around bergschrunds and crevasses, I suddenly realized we had no wands with which to mark our route. A sensation of panic swept me. We might reach the peak and never be able to find a route down. I began cutting arrows in the icy surface, studiously memorizing snow and ice contours, looking back frequently, striving to remember how the route would look on the descent. I reasoned that if we made the ascent rapidly enough, my direction marks would still be intact.

Suddenly Ralph emitted a nondescript whoop and waved his arms. I looked down at him questioningly. How could his enthusiasm be so overflowing when I was so tired? I let it pass.

Finally we gained the ridge we thought to be the summit, only to find the mountain trailing upward to the east. It can't be much farther, I thought. We stopped for a few minutes rest.

"Ralph," I asked, "what were you shouting about down there." I wondered if I looked as haggard as he did. He hesitated a few moments and then answered.

"I thought I saw somebody on the ridge. I guess I was mistaken."

Later I realized that this was the first obvious manifestation of the combined effects of exhaustion, dehydration, and oxygen starvation.

I started moving cautiously up the corniced ridge. It sloped steeply to the north and dropped sheerly to the south. We gained the next ridge, only to find one still higher. I pushed onward, and then, as I topped a snow mound, there it was— the summit. The top of the North American continent was less than a hundred feet from me. The thrill was jarred from me by a tug on my rope. I looked behind just in time to see Ralph stagger and pitch forward into the snow. He lay motionless for a few seconds, struggled to his feet, took a couple uncoordinated steps, and again plunged forward into the snow.

"Ralph," I shouted, "come on. We've only got about fifty feet to go."

He pulled himself to a standing position and muttered through clenched teeth, "Gotta rest." He stumbled backward about ten feet and proceeded to sit on a thin snow cornice overhanging the clouds floating beneath us. I was past the point of terror. I leaned forward heavily on the rope, and he fell forward onto the solid snow.

"Ralph—over here. It's safer." He lifted his head, squinted his eyes several times, and began crawling over to me.

I took him by the shoulders. "Breathe, Ralph, breathe—

deeper, faster—breathe." He began taking deep gulps of air. Within thirty seconds he was again clearheaded.

"Look at what you almost did." He directed his gaze to his tracks, which led from the cornice extending out over the glacier far below us. He shook his head slowly. He reached into his pack and pulled out the silk Century-21 Exposition Flag. I took the flag and started along the last fifty feet of the ridge.

After several steps I turned to Ralph. "Don't move," I said. He nodded.

On the summit was the weathered stump of a bamboo pole, protruding about six inches from the surface. Quickly I tied the flag to this fragment and then stood up. I scratched the names of my wife and children into the snow with my ice axe. An endless sea of clouds surrounded me. I could see nothing else. I had thought for months of the glowing words that would almost spontaneously issue from me when this moment was reached, but no words came. Instead, I felt loneliness. I looked back at Ralph sitting in the snow, and wondered about the trip down. Could we find our way? I thought about the other four of our party, their bitter disappointment. Instead of a sensation of elation, I experienced primarily a sensation of relief—at last I could go home.

I walked down to where Ralph was sitting. He hadn't moved.

"How do you feel?" I asked.

"O.K.," he responded and began to stand up. "I want to plant my foot on the summit now."

"Just a second," I said. I sat down in the snow and looped the rope around my body for a sitting belay.

He started up the last fifty feet. I watched him intently. A careless step could plunge him over the edge. He stood on the summit for a minute perhaps, and then picked his way back.

"Let's go home, Ralph," I shouted. He nodded. "I'd better lead, so I can find my marks in the snow. Before we start down I want you to breathe deeply for a while." He immediately began hyperventilating. We started down.

My arrows and crosses had not yet been erased by the swirling snow. We retraced our route with relative ease, and rather quickly found ourselves at the base of the summit ridge.

Exhaustion now became an overpowering force. I staggered and stumbled along, falling frequently, but always getting up and continuing. I was very much aware of the danger of allowing myself to fall asleep for "a few minutes," with the possibility of awakening hours later, perhaps in a storm. I gave Ralph a central nervous system stimulant and took one myself.

I asked Ralph to lead as we climbed out of the valley since he was more familiar with the route, having covered it an extra time in returning for the stove. He was becoming very quiet. He took the lead, and within about a half hour we had lost the route. We recovered it in a relatively short period, and I again took the lead.

At last we stood looking over Denali Pass and the Harper's Glacier. A blanket of fog had layered down the valley. I knew that our vision would be impaired as we traveled over the glacier, but we had no choice. We moved down to the eighteen thousand foot level and began our retreat down to base camp.

As we advanced into the fog bank, it was as if we had been absorbed by an ethereal mass. I could see nothing except myself. I rubbed my goggles, thinking they must be fogged. No improvement. I took them off. Still no improvement. White pushed out at me from everywhere. There were no shadows. Above, below, to the sides—all the same. I stepped in a strange fashion, feeling for the surface below, not being able to see it. I looked behind me and experienced the strange illusion that Ralph was floating at the end of my rope. He was perfectly clear, but the white below him was identical to the white beside and above him. We were experiencing a total "white-out."

"Ralph," I called, "I can't see a thing. Would you lead for a while?"

"O.K.," he responded.

We changed positions. After a few steps, he shouted back, "I can't see anything either." I knew that he couldn't but in the rear position I felt better able to stop us both if he were to crash into a crevasse. We continued downward.

About an hour later we approached a long crevasse. Ralph cautiously approached the narrowest spot, which looked as if we could jump it easily. He peered into the crevasse, and then began walking parallel to it, stabbing only the tip of his ice axe into the snow and giving it a little twist. The dry snow issued a small creak with each twist. He seemed enormously preoccupied.

I couldn't understand what he was doing, or why, but I knew it was hazardous since a snow-covered side extension of the crevasse would quickly claim him if I didn't stop this.

"Hello down there," he shouted into the crevasse.

"Ralph, what is it?" I asked.

"Jon and Helen are in the cravasse," he said in a very matter-of-fact manner.

"What are they doing?" I inquired. His attitude had tipped me off. He was hallucinating again.

"Oh, just seeking shelter," he answered.

"Ralph, stay right where you are. I'll cross this crevasse and lead awhile."

I moved up to the edge of the crevasse. I had expected Ralph to move out to keep the rope tight, but he had seated himself amid several coils of rope.

I almost asked him to move out to the rope's length, but thought better of it.

"Ralph, could you give me a belay when I jump?" I asked. He began to take up the rope coils in slow motion.

I got ready to jump, and looked toward him for a final check. He had cinched the rope up to me with no slack, so if I jumped I would have been stopped halfway across the crevasse by the rope. I gave the rope a tug, and stripped enough slack from him to complete the jump. I jumped across and put a belay on him. Then he jumped across.

I moved along in the total whiteness, desperately seeking a shadow, a landmark, a familiar ridge or crevasse which would indicate the altitude. But all I saw was nothingness. I was very much concerned over the possibility of us passing the camp and decending too far.

"Listen," Ralph broke the stillness, "I can hear them; they're whispering and laughing."

I bent my head and pulled my parka from my ears, but they were filled only by the cold murmur of the wind. We continued.

Perhaps a half hour later Ralph called to me again. "Do you know what the trouble is?" he asked. "They're hiding from us."

"I don't think so, Ralph," I answered.

"I'm sure of it," he said; "I can hear them."

I was reluctant to disagree with him too vocally, for fear of incurring his hostility. If he became strongly antagonistic I could never get him back to base camp.

A huge bank of crevasses faintly loomed through the fog. I stopped, squinting my eyes and demanding my brain to recall their altitude.

My thoughts were interrupted by some activity on the rope. I turned to see Ralph's empty canteen bottle tumbling toward me, and in another direction, Ralph chasing a rolling flare into a badly crevassed area.

"Ralph, let it go," I ordered. He stopped and looked at me.

"They cost two dollars each," he answered.

"That's O.K., get your canteen," I shouted.

Somewhat reluctantly he turned and headed for his canteen, which had stopped its wild roll. Our plod continued.

It was almost 5 p.m. when Ralph shouted, "Wait."

I stopped and turned to him.

"I can hear the hissing of the stove," he said.

We had now been without food or water for almost thirty hours at an altitude that exerts a tremendous dehydrating effect. We had been without sleep for almost thirty-six hours. I turned away from him and continued walking.

Sometime later I stopped to look at a ridge protruding eerily into my field of vision. I thought we were at about 16,500 feet. If this was correct we were almost to base camp, but I couldn't be sure.

Ralph was sitting in the snow swinging the end of a rope around in front of him, which I thought was one of his sling ropes. His pack was laying in a heap in the snow.

"Come on, Ralph," I said. There was obvious irritation in my voice.

"I have to do something," he answered.

"Don't bother, let's go, it's only a little farther," I lied.

Every time I paused, attempting to determine our location, Ralph would perform some bizarre act. I was becoming increasingly worried about the weather and our physical condition. Even if the weather held, a time was coming when we would be too exhausted and disoriented to rendezvous with the rest of our party. Just how much time we had, I didn't know, but I hated to waste it.

Ralph got up, dropped the rope he had been toying with, and started toward me. A sense of alarm passed through me and I realized he had unroped.

"Ralph," I shouted, "rope up!"

"You said not to bother," he answered.

"Never mind what I said—rope up," I commanded.

He began looping the rope around his waist.

"Put your pack on, too," I shouted.

He looped it over one shoulder and began walking. I almost said something, and then thought if that's the way he wants to carry it, that's his business.

It took several steps before I realized that I couldn't let him travel that way, both because of fatigue and the possible loss of his pack. I stopped and turned toward him. I wondered if I could reason with him.

"Ralph, come here," I called.

He trudged up to me. I grabbed his upper arms and looked into his grizzly face, with an equally grizzly face. I sought his eyes and tried desperately to reach him, deep inside a cave of thirst, hunger, and exhaustion.

"Ralph," I said slowly, emphasizing each word, "we're in trouble." I paused a moment to let it sink in. "We conquered this mountain, but nobody's ever going to know it unless we can find camp. Our only chance is to work together. I need your help." I was hoping that somehow I could reconnect him with reality.

He put his pack on, and we started out again.

A short time later we came upon a small cache of supplies. It was the remains of our camp at 16,350 feet. Apparently our party had decided to drop to a lower altitude. They had said something of this before we separated, so while we were disappointed, we weren't completely surprised. I was sure they would adequately mark the route down from there. Ralph was performing better now. For the first time in untold hours, the tension began to ease somewhat.

We trudged onward, and there in the distance was a red wand marking the route. We continued to follow them, seeing familiar landmarks on the way down to fifteen thousand feet, where we expected to find camp.

And then, through the haze, the faint silhouette of our tents—or was it another illusion?

"Yo!" I hollered.

A muffled but distinct "Yo" floated back to me. We had at last found camp.

We trudged wearily in, sat down, and removed our crampons. We drank a canteenful of water that had been leaning against one of their packs, and we each opened a tin of meat and consumed it greadily. None of our party had come out of the tents, or even spoken a greeting.

Shaking off the snow I crawled into my tent. Ralph crawled into his.

"Hi," I said quietly.

"Hi," Kenn said.

"Hi," said Ron.

I began pulling off my outer clothes. "How's Helen?" I asked.

"Fine," said Kenn. A lot you care, he thought to himself. You guys left her for us to take down. A climbing party should stick together, especially if someone's sick. Some doctor you are.

I finished removing my clothing and crawled into my sleeping bag. God, I was glad Helen was all right; but there was nothing I could do for her as a doctor that anyone else couldn't do. Warmth, food, water, and a lower altitude was what she had required.

Kenn twisted uncomfortably in his sleeping bag and thought of how he could explain his second defeat on Mount Mc-Kinley. Seven hundred feet, he silently grimaced.

I lay there with my eyes open. They hadn't asked if we had reached the summit. I had the feeling they were afraid to ask, for fear we had been successful. I knew their disappointment was intense. I had specifically asked each of them to go to the summit, together or with me. In fact, I had asked them so I could forever be content with the fact that they had had their opportunity. I didn't know why I had to be ashamed about it. If no one had reached the summit, Helen would be blamed, I thought. It was a comfortable rationalization now, but I had never thought of it while climbing. Finally I spoke.

"Kenn, we reached the summit. Somebody had to do it. You know it was only the result of our combined effort that put us there; our expedition is now a successful one."

Several seconds elapsed before he quietly answered.

"Congratulations," he said.

I didn't know if he was sincere or not, but I knew he would never forgive us.

7 ▲
Surrounded By Avalanches

We awakened to a gray day. The weather matched our mood. All of us were suffering the many effects of altitude, fatigue, and frostbite. Our lips were cracked and bleeding. Blisters were beginning to appear on fingertips and toes, the usual aftermath of frostbite. Ralph and I were experiencing the anticlimax, the psychological depression following the completion of an exciting experience, but also the feeling of guilt for being the only members of our party to reach the summit. The rest of the party were undergoing the enormous disappointment of not quite reaching the summit, knowing that their chance was forever gone.

All of us were well aware that we had been expected to reach civilization six days ago. We were becoming uneasy at the prospects of an unnecessary search party being initiated, and the concern of our families.

It was one of those mornings in which the only really powerful urge was to crawl more deeply into the sleeping bag, looking for a retreat that didn't exist.

The morning was almost over when I heard Jon outside preparing breakfast for his tent. I recalled that there were the remains of an igloo at this fifteen-thousand-foot altitude.

"Kenn," I said, "is the igloo sturdy enough to cook in?"

"What igloo?" he replied curiously.

"You know—the igloo," I responded.

"You mean the cave?" he answered.

"Cave? Is there a cave here too?" I said.

He sat up, still in his sleeping bag, and gave me an incredulous look. "What are you talking about?"

I sat up also and looked at him with equal disbelief. I assumed he must be suffering from some mental confusion, but I didn't know how extensive it was.

"Kenn," I started patiently, "the ice cave was back up at 16,350 feet. We're at . . ."

He interrupted me. "That's where we are."

I looked at him for a few seconds, looking for some expression that would tip me off as to whether this was a joke or not. His expression remained unchanged.

"But, Kenn, you moved the camp down to fifteen thousand feet yesterday. Ralph and I found the remains of the old camp, and followed your wands down here."

"We didn't move the camp," Kenn answered. "We're still at 16,350 feet. Take a look if you don't believe me."

I turned around and quickly zipped open the tent flap. I peered out and with confused disbelief found that Kenn was right. Withdrawing into the tent, I sat silently for several seconds searching my mind for the answer. Then, slowly I understood: what Ralph and I had thought to be the remains of camp was actually the food cache we had left on the day before the storm, when the rest of the team had failed to join us. The wands also were left from our ascent. The rest was imagination.

I explained our mistake to Kenn, and he asked me if I was sure that it wasn't just me.

"Ralph," I called.

"Yes," came the alert reply from our other tent.

Although nourishment and rest had caused a complete recovery from the delirium of the previous day, I suspected that Ralph also thought the camp had been moved down to fifteen thousand feet.

"Do you know where we are?" I shouted.

"What?" he shouted back.

"What altitude are we at?" I shouted.

"A little over fifteen thousand," came the reply.

It was well into the afternoon before we had struck camp and were slowly moving downward. Tempers were short and several minor personality skirmishes occurred. Our progress reflected our morale, and we only reached the fifteen-thousand-foot level before we again set up our tents.

By the next morning our team spirit was beginning to return, and we traveled easily over the glacier to the base of Browne's Tower, where we picked up some gear and food we had cached for the trip down.

We were now faced with the descent of The Coxcomb, the name given to the uppermost thousand steep feet of Karsten's Ridge. I looked forward to it with apprehension, but found some solace in the fact that each step downward would not have to be retraced. I found even greater solace in the fact that from now on the temperatures would be kinder. My frostbitten toes were beginning to worry me. Ron had four frostbitten fingers on one hand and three on the other.

I tried to clear my mind. This was the area where years ago Thayer's party had hurtled into the valley below, killing Thayer and severely injuring one of the other members. We squinted suspiciously down the slope as if to judge the malice of our adversary. Kenn cut a wedge of snow loose with his ice axe. It tumbled crazily downward, gathering more snow as it went. The bulk of the avalanche exploded on an outcropping of rock about a thousand feet below us.

"It's ripe for an avalanche," commented Kenn.

No one answered him.

He took the lead and we started down the steep snow pitch. His route was nearly vertical. Traversing back and forth would almost certainly cut an avalanche loose from the slope and bury us deep into the valley.

As he advanced downward, a mound of sliding snow began to gather just below him, growing larger and larger with each step. When it approached the size of an automobile he stopped and looked up at me. I knew that soon we would have to travel through the mound. The chance that our course through it would precipitate a full-scale avalanche seemed almost a certainty. I waited for his decision.

"Give me about fifty feet of slack and anchor in," he shouted; "I'm going to try to cut it loose."

I moved down about fifty feet and anchored myself into the slope as securely as I could with my ice axe. Above me, Ron did the same.

Kenn moved down and began to hack a transverse line immediately above the mound. He hoped that this would provide a sheer line for the avalanche. He knew that he would be caught in it, but if our ropes held, it would roar off around him leaving him dangling on the slope.

Many minutes later Kenn had completed the narrow, ragged trench, but the mound refused to break loose. He signaled for more slack, which I immediately gave him. He moved into the mound and jumped several times. It wouldn't budge.

"It won't go," he shouted.

I had no answer for him.

Cautiously he began to move through it, wondering which second it would pick to catch us vulnerable. Immediately upon passing through the entire mound, he began to diagonally traverse to one side, out of its course. When Ron could no longer act as anchor man, Kenn anchored himself into the slope.

We again began our steep descent. With each plunging step, I would slide several feet, digging my heels into the slope and dragging my ice axe to bring the step to a halt.

Several hundred feet later we approached a relative leveling of the slope, a point where a knifelike ridge extends downward. It seemed a relief to have a different problem to cope with. We stopped to rest, and looked up at Jon, Helen, and Ralph negotiating the areas we had just traveled.

About thirty minutes later, they wearily plodded over to

our position and sat heavily into the snow. Few words were exchanged, but we knew we shared common thoughts. We gazed down Karsten's Ridge—two miles of hazard extending like the tail of a great white lizard, finally disappearing into the glacier below.

Kenn laboriously got up, stretched a bit, and started methodically down the ridge. I knew I had several minutes before the rope grew taut. I took a quick sip of water flavored with fruit powder; my blistered lips jarred me, and rising to my feet I followed.

We had gone about a hundred yards when the quiet cold air was pierced by a shout.

"Falling!"

Instantaneously, with a flash of steel, I drove my ice axe into the ridge, slamming a braced foot against the shaft and looping a coil of rope around it. Kenn was sliding in a small cloud of ice crystals kicked up by his axe, fighting for a hold on the bare ice. The rope came tight against my axe, and the small crystal cloud settled around him. For several seconds he didn't move. Then he spoke, "Thank you."

"It's truly a pleasure," I answered.

As we moved on down the ridge I was comforted by the realization that we had left fixed ropes over the steepest, most exposed areas of Karsten's Ridge. We were approaching such an area now. Every twenty feet or so Kenn took a deep sweep with his ice axe in an effort to pick up the rope, which had been buried by snow since our ascent. With one of his sweeps he pulled it up, clipped a carabiner to it, and proceeded with greater confidence. I followed suit when I reached the frozen rope. Jon, bringing up the rear, attempted to extract the snow pickets wherever possible, since there was always the chance that we might have further need for them during our descent. The partly buried fixed rope was abandoned.

At thirteen thousand feet my attention was attracted to the rapid fluttering of a bird several hundred feet above us. It appeared to be a seagull or maybe a hawk. It was the first life I had seen since the solitary raven above our airdrop camp. I wondered what possible reason he could have for his high sojourn, and immediately reflected that he could have similar thoughts about us.

Every now and then I would cut a wedge of snow loose from the ridge and watch it gather into avalanche proportions as it bounced crazily down the slope. Frequently nothing more than my footstep was necessary to trigger an avalanche.

We had come to one of the steepest snow pitches on the ridge, but it was only about three-hundred-feet long, and we had "already put in our sweat on this pitch," I thought, as I remembered the fixed rope Ron and I had strung while the rest of the party had set up camp on the only wide area on Karsten's Ridge. Kenn had stopped in the thigh-deep snow and was digging. I thought he was clearing a spot out of the wind for a rest. I was a little irritated because I was stuck in an uncomfortable place on the side of the ridge, but then that's the way it goes, I thought.

I stuck a piece of hard candy into my mouth. God, but you get sick of the insipid taste of hard candy. The mixed salted nuts tasted good, but the ensuing pain in my cracked, blistered lips made me wonder if the torture was worthwhile.

There was almost no wind on the ridge now. It was as if the world had stopped. I looked around at the snow-covered peaks surrounding us. On the vertical faces a cross section of the mountain was visible—a couple hundred feet of snow overlaying about fifty feet of slate which was being pushed up by the reddish-gray granite spires.

Wasn't Kenn through with his rest yet? What was he doing? As these thoughts passed through my mind, he stood up and threw up his hands. He shouted something which was carried off by the wind before I could hear.

"What?" I shouted back.

"—can't find—rope—have to go without."

Enough of the words came through to tell the story. He

had been digging, not resting, trying to find the snow picket and the attached rope, but he couldn't dig down to them. They were deeper than the three feet he had dug. The first and last part of this pitch would be safe, since Ron could anchor us securely part of the way, and Kenn could do the anchoring when he reached the nearly level area at the end of the traverse. However, I knew there would be at least fifty feet in the middle when all three of us would cling to the surface with a zero margin of safety.

We started down. If one of us slipped during the critical period, I knew that nothing could prevent all three of us from disappearing forever down the several thousand feet into the glacial valley. My only concern was that I wouldn't be the one to initiate such a chain of events.

At our former Karsten's Ridge camp we rested and talked for about thirty minutes. We were about halfway down the ridge now, with the most difficult part above and now behind us. I found myself almost reveling in the idea.

Suddenly we were startled by a gigantic shaking of the ridge under us, followed by a muffled boom echoing around the canyon walls. I wondered for several wild seconds if part of the ridge would crumble into the valley, but the episode was brief. We casually argued as to whether the glacier had shifted, or whether this had been a true earthquake. We knew that there was an earthquake fault located in the vicinity of Mount McKinley. I finally settled the discussion with the comment that either way, it was just another routine crisis. We moved on.

Perhaps an hour later we had come to our last string of fixed rope. We uncovered it without difficulty and I clutched it with my left hand to steady myself. As I was traversing a particularly narrow bit of ridge with a sheer icy cliff on one side, the snow under my right foot gave way. I plummeted to the right and backward over the cliff, shouting "Falling" as I went. Fortunately, I had a death grip on the fixed rope;

I was spun upside down by the pack weight which had pulled off one shoulder, and I hung plastered against the wall.

There was little danger, but it seemed damnably inconvenient. I hung there a few seconds regaining my wind, and then finally with accumulated strength and a supreme effort, I righted myself. With one hand steadying myself on the rope to prevent my being inverted again, I used the other to gradually chip toeholds out of the ice with my ice axe. In this manner I eventually gained the ridge again. Ron had been in belay position in the event that I would require his help. I thanked him and signaled for him to remove his belay.

"Some people will go to any extreme to gain a unique view," he commented.

An hour or two later found us at the point where we had first gained the ridge. I reflected for a few moments on the events that had taken place since I last stood on that spot. We descended uneventfully into the valley and reclaimed our snowshoes, which stood like a welcoming committee where we had stuck them. As we settled for a rest, an overwhelming fatigue had caught up to me. But I drowsed comfortably in the knowledge that at least we now had the exposed ridges behind us.

8 ▲
THE DESCENT

WE WERE AWAKENED by Jon wafting a bowl of hot stew laced with caribou pemican under our noses. It tasted unbelievably good. In my sleepy hunger I felt that I owed him a debt so large that I might never be able to adequately repay him. The snow had become deep and soft here, so we packed our crampons away; from now on we would descend on snowshoes.

After our nap and nourishment we were moving down the mountain at a decent pace, but I worried a little about Jon. He had cooked while the rest of us slept. Would this catch up with him later? I filed it in my mind.

Most of the glacier traveling was rather routine now. Keep ropes taut, probe suspicious area, travel until you're sure you can't take another step, then rest a minute or two, and walk again. Step over most crevasses, jump others, down into some huge ones, and up the other side—on and on.

The crevasses had increased in width since our last passage over them. Several marked with wands where we had jumped, now gaped widely out of jumping range. New routes were explored and found, but always with the reassuring knowledge that we didn't have to return to lug equipment over them, as we had done during the ascent.

Many times I looked back on Karsten's Ridge, building a permanent mental image of the snow billowing along its windswept edge, silhouetted against the bluest of blue skies, and its foreboding slopes rising to the Harper's Glacier like a stairway. I felt an inner thrill that I had been there and returned.

Jon was leading now, stepping, probing with our eight-foot probing pole, withdrawing the pole, another careful step, maybe a sideways step, looking, listening, like some giant insect moving a feeler through this forest of gnarled ice.

As time passed, fatigue was becoming a more constant companion, and a more difficult one to shake for more than short periods. It was after midnight and we were enshrouded in dense clouds when our exhausted rope teams were passing under the immense hanging ice cliffs on the east wall. We were forced to pass under them, as we did on our ascent, because our attempts to find an alternate route had failed. I felt an enormous uneasiness, but it couldn't be helped. I knew that we were traveling slower and slower, but we were doing the best we could.

Jon finally sat exhausted in the snow. I was stunned when he began making an earnest plea for camping right there, ignoring the mountainous icy cornices hanging over us. It took many minutes to dissuade him. I recalled his lack of rest. Kenn picked up the lead.

By two in the morning we had traveled toward the center of the glacier, clear of the avalanche danger, and virtually free of crevasses. We had to be getting close to our airdrop camp. Ron and I voted to continue until we reached the old site. The rest voted against us, and we wearily set up our tents.

The fog had cleared during the early morning hours, and we were greeted by a bright crispness in the air. We packed our gear and headed for the food cache at our airdrop site. Our trip down so far had been hurried, and with little attention to nutrition. Much food had been abandoned to ease the carrying load. We keenly looked forward to a meal of variety and volume.

We crested the small knoll at seventy-two hundred feet

that had been our campsite, and broke out our shovels. Snow had covered our mound of supplies during our seventeen-day absence. We dug quietly at first, and finally vigorously with a shocked realization that our supplies had been attacked by something. We dug through the snow only to find our food packages ripped and scattered. Piling the unbroken canned goods in the snow, we sat in mournful silence. There were no tracks or droppings to indicate our tormentor, the destruction probably having been done weeks ago. We assumed that a wolverine or perhaps a flock of huge ravens had done the damage. We knew that a wolverine had been following us toward the mountain, but we had thought he had stopped when we moved onto the glacier at five thousand feet.

We prepared a stew from what remained and tried to enjoy our last meal, knowing that we wouldn't reach civilization for at least two days.

Leaving the glacier, we were now traversing the steep side of the ridge paralleling the glacial valley. Avalanche hazard was also extreme in this location. Moving along as rapidly as we could, we stole furtive glances upward at the huge, over-hanging ice cliffs, listening for any sound that might warn us of its downfall. An avalanching fragment alone would be sufficient to sweep us into the gaping crevasses below us.

As I carefully slammed each boot into the slope to gain footing, I wondered if the mountain would allow us to pass these ramparts, or would it hurl a final bombardment of snow and ice to forever hide this conquest of its summit?

The tension grew as our two rope teams were strung out along the slope. Jon, Helen, and Ralph were perhaps a hundred yards ahead of us, out of sight most of the time due to the irregularity of the slope.

"Hold up," shouted Kenn, "I've got to fix a boot."

I dreaded the pause under the menacing ice wall hanging above us, but I knew Kenn hated it equally. Several hour-long minutes passed while he solved his problem. As he stood up to signal his O.K., a thunderous roar filled the air. Part of the hanging cliff had broken loose, starting a tumbling, crushing avalanche. We prepared to jettison our packs, but then it became evident that the avalanche course would pass several yards ahead of us. We froze in our tracks, awaiting the end of the fury, realizing that Kenn's short pause had probably saved our lives.

But what of our other rope team? They were almost directly in its path. Their footprints had disappeared into the icy rubble.

"Yaooo," shouted Kenn in almost a yodel.

We listened for a reply. Nothing but the tinkle of ice particles tumbling over the now quiet avalanche debris.

"Yaooo," Kenn shouted again.

Only quiet. Had our expedition ended in a final tragedy? And then, "Yaooo," in the distance.

Quickly we moved out to join them. When we caught up, we were no longer under the hanging ice walls. Jon explained how the avalanche had broken loose directly above them, roared down, and was diverted to either side of them by a large rocky prominence. Our best and most apt comment was a slow shake of the head and a smile.

As we continued on we came upon the solitary tracks of a wolverine. We wished him no good.

The going was fairly easy now, and we were almost to the point where we would return to the glacier. Suddenly I stopped. My attention had been drawn to a small glistening puddle about the size of a grapefruit. I knelt to examine it. I placed a bare finger in the water and gave it a quick stir. It was the first naturally occurring water in three weeks. It seemed like years. I knew the image would find its way into the indelible portions of my memory. The rope was tightening. Quickly I stood up and moved on. We had only a few more miles of glacier now; crevasses were few and of minimal significance. The danger had melted into little more than a long slog.

The foot-weary hours passed slowly. At five thousand feet

we finally left the Muldrow Glacier. The surrounding hills were no longer snow-covered. It had been three weeks since we first looked hopefully up the glacier toward the mountain. Tiny alpine flowers had bloomed in all their varicolored enthusiasm. I felt as if I had returned to the earth I knew and loved.

We unroped and removed our snowshoes. I felt an incredible feeling of freedom in being able to walk without the annoyance of rope handling, and with neither the weight of snowshoes nor crampons to burden me. We walked as far as we could, and finally crawled exhausted into our sleeping bags beside a gurgling stream to remind us that we were off the mountain.

Seven hours of refreshing, danger-free sleep had charged us with enthusiasm for the twenty-five miles of green wet grasslands, hills, and rivers between us and our destination at Wonder Lake. We stuffed our sleeping bags into our packs and were quickly on the move, but not before donning our mosquito head nets. Although we had exchanged our frigid, odorless, colorless world of snow boredom for one of warmth, fresh smells, and spectral color, we had accepted mosquitoes in the trade—thousands of hungry mosquitoes. Swarms followed us continuously, necessitating a slightly louder conversational tone to be heard over the unrelenting buzzing. The occasional mosquito getting inside the head net was vulnerable to the snapping of a food-short mountaineer.

Since we were covered all the time, we wouldn't bother to strike at them unless a kill of at least four was in the offing. We began to make a game of it when I announced a kill of seven with one slap. Ground rules were quickly established. Dead mosquitoes were counted on the struck surface and on the striking hand, while a slight blowing through pursed lips prevented new live ones from fouling up the official count. Jon stole my thunder with a record of seventeen. The record passed around several times before falling to Ron with a tally of twenty-one mosquitoes with one slap.

As the hours and miles passed by, I wondered if I would have to readjust to civilization. The thought occurred to me that I might be tempted to carry a wad of toilet paper in my pocket, and go when and where the urge struck me, as I had for the last month—a month without plumbing, beds, baths, music, coffee, or news of civilization. I wondered if I would ever lose the keen appreciation of the beauty and tranquility of the world I had returned to.

Many of the streams we were crossing now had flecks of gold rolling haphazardly along the edges.

In the distance I heard a faint roar. The mighty McKinley River was announcing itself. I knew we would reach it after a mile or two of thrashing through the willow swamps. We had passed across the snout of the Muldrow Glacier during our ascent of the mountain, and with the late spring had only had to cross several small tributaries of the river.

By midnight we stood on the banks of this gigantic river—a mile-wide torrent of rushing, gurgling, frigid water generated from melting ice, filled with rocky, glacial silt and occasional pieces of bobbing ice. Its expanse was laced with sandbars every couple hundred feet. I smiled as I thought of the many parties which had been frustrated by this huge moat and had never even completed their approach to the mountain. However, to us its formidable barrier was dampened somewhat by what we had already experienced. I knew that generally it was no more than mid-thigh or waist deep, unless one of us were unlucky enough to drop into a hole.

We would have to cross it with our packs loose. If we stumbled we would probably experience no more than a freezing ducking, and quite likely the loss of a pack, but it didn't seem to constitute a threat to life.

We searched the banks until each of us possessed a sturdy pole to use as an upstream brace to assist our crossing. I sat in the sand and removed my heavy boots, coarse socks, and wool pants. I slipped into my nylon windpants and replaced the rubber boots. My wool pants and socks were crammed into the top of my pack. Heaving my pack onto my back, leaving the waist strap dangling, I trudged to the edge of the current with my rough pole grasped firmly. I was ready.

The first almost painful sensation as the icy water poured into my boots was followed by a series of thoughts and instructions to myself: lean heavily against the staff, keep moving, can't stay in one spot long, water washes footing out, slipping! Move another foot, quick! Annoying goose flesh sensations when I almost fell. Getting deeper, better try another direction. End of staff stuck in rocks. Careful. There, its dislodged. Move it over. So far so good. More than halfway now. Feet getting numb, cold. Getting shallower now. Foot sinking in mud. Ease it out. That's it, don't let your pack slip and throw you off balance. Don't fall now. Steady. Almost over. At last—God, but my feet are cold.

We walked up and down the sandbar, looking for a likely crossing to the next sandbar. Then, carefully into the chilling, gritty water, and another crossing, and another sandbar, and so on until a mile of rushing, frequently white water interspersed with rocky bars had been forded.

Sitting heavily upon the bank, I quickly dumped the icy water from my boots. My wool pants, socks, and then my boots were pulled back on over the shivering wet legs. I tied my windpants to the back of my pack to dry, and took some moments to gaze back at the mountain. My eyelids began to droop heavily as fatigue overtook me. I jerked my head suddenly. Can't let up quite yet, I thought.

We were about to enter a forest of black spruce; about six miles would see us plod wearily into the ranger station at Wonder Lake to announce our survival. This might be my last opportunity for a final look at the mountain.

As I watched, a huge bank of clouds suddenly shielded the mountain from my view, as if to draw the curtain on our adventure. My mind was wandering over the many moods of Mount McKinley: Denali, the great one, the intense burning heat, the bitter cold, the ripping wind, the quiet, the gentleness, the awesome magnitude will continue though no eyes, no senses now perceive its might.

PART
TWO

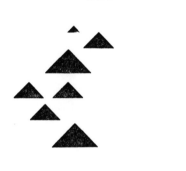

ACONCAGUA

9 ▲
Just One More

"Dad, is this the big mountain you climbed?"

My two small sons thrust an open encyclopedia onto my lap and climbed in after it. It had been several months since I had returned from Mount McKinley. Weary and frostbitten, I had sworn off expedition mountaineering, and I felt no different now. The cracked lips, sore nostrils, and peeling skin disappeared after a couple weeks, as did the insatiable appetite and thirst. The increased cold sensitivity and the tingly numb feeling in my toes and fingertips had continued.

I looked at the photograph. It was an aerial view of a portion of the Andes with one gigantic mass looming above the rest—Mount Aconcagua, at twenty-three thousand feet, the highest point in the Western Hemisphere.

"No boys. That isn't the mountain I climbed."

At that moment a seed was planted.

As the months went by the seed grew. The effects of the frostbite left from my Mount McKinley expedition disappeared in eight or nine months. It wasn't long after that that I ran into Ralph Mackey again. I rather casually mentioned the possibility of some mountaineering in the Andes. He said he would check on the round-trip fare to Argentina, just out of curiosity. Following this I noticed a distinct coolness in his wife's attitude toward me for a period of time.

While having lunch with Ralph a few months later, we got to talking about the cost of such a trip. We decided that we already possessed practically all the necessary expedition equipment. We agreed that food would cost us less than if we stayed home.

"Ralph, it certainly seems a shame to allow our expedition gear to gather dust and mold."

"Wasteful."

"Almost criminal," I added.

"I checked on the round-trip fare. It's only about eight hundred dollars."

"I don't see how we can afford not to go."

We immediately composed a letter which we sent to the Argentine Embassy in Washington, D.C.

After several months we received a meager but enthusiastic reply stating that they appreciated our interest and would like to be of help. We followed up with a letter again asking for information as to permission, maps, and so forth.

A couple of months elapsed before we received another reply: "We appreciate your interest and would like to be of help"—but still no help.

However, in the meantime we had also contacted the U.S. Embassy in Argentina. They had given us the address of Vincente Cicchitti, a professor of Greek History and Philosophy at the University of Mendoza. Professor Cicchitti, a forty-six-year-old bachelor, is a very learned man, known and respected throughout western Argentina. Besides his native Spanish, he speaks French, Italian, and English. Our letters to him were promptly answered, and from then on we had access to information about the mountain. We found that he had been a member of an expedition to Dhaulageri in the Himalayas many years ago. He had climbed Tupungato, the second highest peak in the Andes, and Aconcagua by the usual route some sixteen years ago. He expressed interest in joining us, preferably in establishing a new route. We offered him an enthusiastic affirmation.

Events were now moving at a sufficient pace to warrant putting the rest of the party together. Ralph and I conferred. I suggested Dick Hill, who had almost gone with us up

McKinley. A thirty-three-year-old bachelor, doctor of medicine, he lived by himself in a rented bungalow in Seattle, the interior of which was littered beyond description with scientific books and journals, pieces of electronic equipment, fragments of motors and radios, and bits of climbing gear. It was overseen by a tomcat named Fleishecker who maintained access through an open window. Parked in front of the house was a small car, littered much like the house; parked in the garage was a motorcycle capable of speeds in excess of one hundred miles per hour. Dick customarily abandoned both in favor of his bicycle, which he pedaled two miles to the University of Washington Medical School in order to spend the day and sometimes the night in research laboratories, littered like his car and house.

Dick was the only one of us without any expedition experience, but also the only one who had done much solo climbing. I offered him a spot with us; he agreed to go if I led the expedition, a dubious honor I had been trying to avoid after noting Kenn's troubles on McKinley. Dick was probably the most confirmed bachelor I have ever known, and yet he married six months before we left.

While wondering where we would be able to gain a couple more experienced mountaineers to round out our party, we received the following letter:

May 6, 1964

Dear Ralph and Gene:

Bill Dougall and I have pretty well decided to undertake an ascent of Aconcagua next winter. Bill is leaving for Chile in early June and so time will rapidly fly by for preparations.

In view of your interest, I wondered if it might be possible to join forces and would suggest that we hold a meeting for this purpose.

I am also interested in the Cordilla Blanca area. At the very least we could accomplish some good by exchange of information.

I would like to suggest that we hold a meeting at my home on Thursday, May 14, at 8:00 p.m. I am also available on the prior Tuesday and Wednesday. However, I suggest this date as a time certain.

Please let me know whether you are interested in attending such a meeting and if the date meets with your approval.

Yours very truly,
Paul M. Williams

Our party had crystallized!

While I knew Bill Dougall and Paul Williams only slightly, I was aware of their reputations as highly competent and experienced mountaineers.

Paul Williams is a forty-two-year-old practicing attorney in Seattle, married, with seven children. For several years he directed the Mountain Rescue Council in Seattle, and is still one of their most skilled and active participants. Paul climbed Mount McKinley in 1960. An accomplished ski racer himself, he is a timer licensed by the Pacific Northwest Ski Association. In fact, he served as the Chief Starter for the 1965 National Ski Championship at Crystal Mountain, Washington.

Bill Dougall, forty-three years old, flew fighter missions off an aircraft carrier in World War II, and was credited with the destruction of a Japanese Zero in aerial combat. Having degrees in mathematics and aeronautical engineering, he had given up his work in the aircraft industry some years ago in preference for teaching in a private school, where he stated he could exert more independence. Frankly, I have always suspected that he would do almost anything to have his summers free for unobstructed mountaineering.

Apparently the teaching did not always allow enough independence either, because in early June he took a year's leave of absence in order to take a teaching position in an English School in Santiago, Chile. Of course, it was just a coincidence that Santiago is quite close to Mount Aconcagua.

In typical Dougall style, he bundled his wife and four children into a pickup-camper and proceeded to drive the almost seven thousand miles to Chile.

When he and his family arrived in Panama, he began to put a plan into effect, a plan which he had shared with us in the strictest confidence one night while planning our expedition.

"Say, honey, I've just thought of a great idea," he began. He suggested that they place the auto on board ship and cruise to Chile. At first his wife was skeptical, but he convinced her that the sea trip would be most enjoyable.

"You won't have any trouble handling the kids at all, I'm sure." She gave him a quizzical look.

Then he announced that he was going to fly and meet her there! Why? Well, he was going to have to take a slightly devious route. Since he spoke fluent French, he had been asked to lead a French-American expedition on Mount Ararat in Turkey in search of Noah's Ark, a church-financed expedition. He arrived in Santiago a little late, but in time to enter his teaching post. Incidentally, he did not find Noah's Ark.

Those of us remaining—Ralph, Dick, Paul, and myself—began planning and buying group equipment and food. Our plan was to be one of the best prepared expeditions ever to face the mountain. Two months prior to our departure we crated our carefully chosen food and gear and placed it on a Norwegian Freighter bound for Valparaiso, Chile.

We plunged into our training program two to three months before leaving. Since we were not planning on carrying any oxygen, it was especially important to gain as much as possible from our training schedule. Mine consisted primarily of three trips weekly to the gym to engage in five hundred rope skips, three hundred deep knee bends, fifty situps, twenty-five pushups, bag punching, and then into the swimming pool for six quick laps. Occasionally I would run five-mile distances to vary the routine.

We gathered for a final meeting before our December 27th flight departure date and studied what photographs and maps we had been able to cull from several sources—French, German, Spanish, and English. Our tentative plan was to rendezvous with Bill Dougall in Santiago, pick up our expedition equipment in the port of Valparaiso, and travel with it by train across the Andes to Puente del Inca, Argentina, where Cicchitti would be waiting for us. He would arrange a mule caravan to transport our expedition twenty-seven miles to base camp.

We drank a toast to the mountain and to our success on it.

10 ▲
Mula!

As our airplane circled to land at Santiago, Chile, my mind flashed back over the days since we had left Seattle. We had had difficulties almost since the beginning. Our first problem occurred when an engine failed on our aircraft and we were forced to change planes in San Francisco.

While changing airlines in Mexico City, our baggage was found to be overweight, requiring an additional twenty-five dollars. We solved this problem by unpacking our enormously heavy Eiger boots. We sat down on the floor of the airline terminal and proceeded to put them on, amid curious and amused bystanders. The ticket agent quickly waved us through.

We got off the airplane and met Bill Dougall as planned.

As we cruised along in Bill's Volkswagen bus, Paul asked what had happened to the pickup-camper he left Seattle with.

"Couldn't afford it. Do you know that import duty on cars is five hundred percent? A three thousand dollar car would cost over fifteen thousand dollars!"

It was clear why there was no such thing as an automobile junkyard in Chile. No car could be so old, or so wrecked that it was not cheaper to fix it than to buy a new one. I began to notice absolutely beautiful vintage cars on the road—German, French, English, Italian, and American.

We were heading up one of the side hills now, approaching Bill's home. We twisted through rows of trees, a long driveway, and finally his house came into view. It was a three-story, white, Spanish bungalow with a delightful view of the city and mountains. The grounds and orchard were magnificent. A swimming pool nestled near the house. There were numerous balconies, innumerable bedrooms, three bathrooms all with bidets, and two with sunken tubs.

"How about making this base camp?" Paul joked.

"I didn't know you were among the filthy rich," Ralph added.

"Not bad for about two hundred dollars a month, is it?" Bill replied.

"Two hundred a month? You're kidding."

"No; that includes a full-time gardener."

"You mean you have to pay extra for the maid? How tragic."

"Yeah," he smiled. "Her hours are 8 a.m. to 10 p.m. She gets twenty-three dollars a month."

The following morning we got up early and headed for Valparaiso (Veil of Paradise) to pick up our expedition gear. We arrived at the port authority and ran headlong into disappointment and frustration. This was immediately followed by more of the same with the customs officials, the shipping company, and finally the Federal Government. It became apparent that no one had the least idea what had happened to our expedition gear. Our gear was either lost on the docks, stolen, back in Seattle, still on the ship, lost at sea, or some combination thereof. It became obvious that we would have to either abandon our assault or face the mountain with what we could borrow. And one of our strongest reassurances in planning this climb was that we were approaching the mountain as undoubtedly the best-equipped expedition ever to challenge the summit.

Fortunately, we had carried our packboards and boots. But we were missing everything else: down clothing, sleeping bags, food, tents, stoves, fuel, medical supplies, ropes, and hardware. The months of planning and accumulating the proper equipment had all been in vain.

We sat around Dougall's table, a badly depressed group of climbers, but not yet ready to abandon our expedition.

"What are the chances of buying some of the equipment locally, Bill?"

"Even if we could afford it, the answer is an absolute negative. Mountaineering equipment doesn't exist in stores down here. Practically the only mountaineers are the crazy foreigners." He threw a piece of paper and a pencil onto the table.

"Let's start over," he said. "What do we really need?"

We began making a list of the absolute barest essentials disregarding both comfort and safety. Bill dragged out all his odds and ends of equipment, and then got on the phone and began calling climbers in Santiago, the most notable being George Lowe, son-in-law of Sir John Hunt. George had accompanied Sir John on the first successful Mount Everest Expedition, and is presently the headmaster of a Santiago school.

While sipping tea with George, his wife Susan, and Lady Hunt, he explained that we were welcome to any equipment he had, but there was not quite enough to outfit two people.

We began filling our essential list with a patchwork array of items. I ended up with no down clothing of any kind and an old sleeping bag with snaps down the side. Ralph had accepted the loan of Lucy Dougall's knickers.

Hardware was completely unavailable, but we had reformed a nucleus of essential equipment. What had started out as probably the best-equipped expedition ever to face the mountain had suddenly degenerated into one of the most ill-equipped.

On New Year's Eve we decided to forget our problems and attend a dinner party at the home of one of the American Embassy officials. While at the party several of us began to worry a little about Dick Hill's personality. A brilliant fellow, he so loves an intellectual argument that he is liabe to take any stand, no matter how untenable or unbelievable, in order to foment one. In an effort to find an adversary I have heard him argue eloquently for causes he vehemently opposes. The seating arrangements were quietly made to place him next to the American Peace Corps representative. We felt that at least this individual was specially trained to be peaceable. War broke out an hour later, and wasn't resolved until the Peace Corps man angrily left the table and went home.

Unable to forget our equipment loss, a couple of us struck up an acquaintance with an attorney working in the Chilean State Department. We poured our problems into his patient ears, explaining that the ship (*Eidanger*) had failed to off-load our equipment. To our amazement, he made an appointment for us with the Attorney General at the Casa de Moneda (Capitol Building) in the morning.

The next day found us being escorted by our newfound friend past armed guard after guard, through elaborate hallways, up marble staircases to a great oak door bearing the inscription, "Abogado de Jefe."

After appropriate introductions, our problems were translated to the Attorney General. He immediately got on the telephone and called the Secretary of the Navy, who ordered the ship to return to port to deliver our equipment. He announced this would take a few days.

All the way back to Dougall's house we talked of the power of important friends and connections, of surprised shippers— "that'll teach 'em," etc.

The next morning we included this new windfall into our revised plans. Paul and Bill volunteered to stay behind to receive our gear from the ship when it returned to port in Valparaiso. Ralph, Dick and I would proceed to Puente del Inca to meet Vincente and get the rest of the plans underway. We had lost too much time already.

Lucy Dougall drove us to the train station, and we ran headlong into a new kind of crisis—a train strike.

"You mean we can't get over the Andes into Argentina?"

"Not by train, Senor."

"Good grief, Charlie Brown."

"What, Senor?"

"Never mind."

Lucy Dougall spoke fluent Spanish, and knew her way around the intricacies of the Latin mind.

"What now, Lucy?"

"There's a road over the mountains."

"You don't mean . . . ?"

"Why not?"

We looked at each other, shrugged our shoulders and answered, "Indeed, why not?"

Lucy hailed a taxicab, talked intently with the driver for awhile with much gesticulating. She walked back to us with a very self-satisfied expression.

"Ten dollars apiece, and you leave immediately."

"That's cheaper than the train!"

"And more exciting too," she added ominously. "Never underestimate the power of a woman."

"I never have."

We thanked her, said goodbye, and roared off, narrowly averting several collisions before losing sight of the train station. The trip was certainly exciting. We decided that we had one of the truly great taxi drivers. He would never yield. We dubbed him Barney (after Oldfield). I wondered if we would find anything more hazardous on the mountain.

As our caravan twisted its way up the rock-strewn Horcones Valley, now and then dipping into icy streams, our expedition was finally underway—the first American Expedition to Mount Aconcagua, the twenty-three thousand foot summit of the Western Hemisphere.

see p. 93

Hackett in 1949

Jogging along on the back of a mule, my mind wandered over the last week. We had finally crossed the border into Argentina. The customs officials spoke no English. In my broken Spanish I had explained that we were going to climb Mount Aconcagua with Professor Cicchitti from Mendoza.

Apparently they had been forewarned, since they passed all our luggage without opening anything, but only after having us untie it and take it all down from the roof. I had told them that two Americans would pass through in a couple days with two large boxes of supplies, in an effort to prepare them.

Paul and Bill had come through in two days all right, but with no boxes. The ship that had returned to port under order of the Secretary of the Navy was the *Eilanger*, the sister ship of the *Eidanger* carrying our supplies. Amazing how much trouble a little error in pronunciation can cause.

My thoughts were nudged back to the present by the shouts of "Mula," as our wizened, weathered mule skinner pitched his will against that of the mules. Long ago the mule replaced the llama as the South American work animal because of his incredible endurance and tenacity. But even so, the trail is scattered with mule bones—mute testimony to the hardships encountered during the heavily laden journey from nine thousand to thirteen thousand feet. I had been impressed by the small cemetery near Puente del Inca containing the bodies of mountaineers killed on Aconcagua and nearby peaks—men from Europe, North and South America. Where the mule hardships end, the human hardships begin.

The strains of harmonica music and singing arose as Bill and Vincente joined in a French ballad. They were interrupted by a dart of motion across the trail.

"What's that?" Ralph shouted.

A small, tailless, deerlike animal dashed up a hillside and out of sight.

"An agouti," answered Vincente. "They are actually a kind of camel, very shy. I have been told that the bones of one were once found near the summit of Aconcagua, dropped by a condor."

The mountain was beginning to loom enormously between lesser peaks as we progressed. As my eyes traveled the cliffs, I wondered about other climbers up there. At Puente del Inca we had met three dark, robust young men in sport coats with blazers identifying them as Mexican *alpinistas*. One of them identified himself as the leader, Father Fernando de la Mora. He spoke perfect English. They were all from Mexico City, and had climbed the high peaks in Mexico—peaks of about eighteen thousand feet. We had inspected each other's equipment and shared our plans of conquest. The priest had explained that he had climbed Mount Aconcagua by the conventional route a few years previously. They were planning an ascent up a northern glacier route. They had departed three days before us.

I had heard that there was an Argentine party preparing an ascent, and also two German climbers in the area looking for a party to join. I wondered why so few Americans had been on the mountain. On three occasions a solitary American had joined expeditions on this mountain. One had died at Plaza de Mulas of pulmonary edema, another had died on the descent, and the third, William Hackett of Portland, had later been decorated by Dictator Juan Perón.

A cloud of dust ahead signaled trouble as a mule collapsed into the trail, kicking and thrashing. For a while I thought he was having a convulsion, but I doubt if the mule skinner would have allowed it.

"Mula!" he shouted in his hoarse voice. He dismounted from his own mule and, by means of Argentine threats and curses, persuaded the mule that life would be easier carrying his load than laying in the trail.

The walls of the valley were beginning to rise more precipitously. The colossal masses of stratified rock, glazed with hues of purple and gold helped dispel the nagging aches that were developing as we continued the twenty-seven mile journey toward our base camp. I couldn't complain about the thick sheepskin saddle, but the aching in my knees was shouting for a change in position.

I got off the mule and led him for about a half mile, figuring it would be good for both of us. I wondered if he perceived the scattered mule bones as being of his kind, and if so, did they discourage him or push him onward. I climbed back into my saddle and continued the journey to base camp.

Although Aconcagua has been climbed many times, only three ascents have been made by other than the conventional route. Polish, Swiss, and French expeditions made these deviations. The most recent of these was in the early 1950s. Our eyes searched the mountain as if we could force it to relinquish the secret of a new route. However, we knew our lack of hardware would seriously hamper us.

I cast an appraising eye up the West Face. How had I ever been talked into attempting an unexplored route when the "Sentinel of Stone," as the Incas called it, had already claimed thirty-two lives by the conventional route?

11 ▲
Base Camp

As our mules crested the last rise completing the nine-hour trek, the area known as Plaza de Mulas spread out before us. This consisted of several rocky acres of relatively level terrain situated between the north end of the abrupt West Face and the Upper Horcones Glacier. A small wooden shelter hut secured by stout guy wires squatted near a pile of rocks. Near it an elaborate device for measuring precipitation had been constructed, but it was unmanned and unused.

As our weary mules clomped into camp, Vincente's four friends began waving wildly to us. They had preceded us by a day, and intended to enjoy the adventure from the vantage point of base camp. Vincente's sister, a nurse, was frustrated in her exuberance by her lack of English, although her greetings were put into polite English by a small, quiet Argentine librarian. An Argentine opera singer and a Chilean political science student seemed to complete our welcoming committee. But not quite—a medium-size dog came barking from around the hut. At thirteen thousand feet, one of the highest living dogs in the world, he spent the summer subsisting on scraps offered him by climbers. When winter approached he accompanied the mule skinner back down to Puente del Inca.

As we unloaded our equipment, the mule skinner pulled some hay from a pile of bales stacked near the hut, in order to feed his mules before heading down. As he tumbled a bale from the pile, several tiny large-eared mice scurried for cover. These little fellows were quite bold when it came to eating.

Unless shooed away, they would even attempt to crawl into a pocket for a morsel. The following day one made a daring raid across my leg, snatched a cookie resting on my knee, and made a clean getaway.

Before erecting our tents we examined the shelter hut. Argentine Mountain Troops had erected this prefabricated structure. It was about fifteen feet long and ten feet wide with beams crisscrossing the inside, preventing anything but stooped-over walking. Much of the inside was covered with penciled notations from previous expeditions—Peruvian, Chilean, Argentine, German, Mexican, and Polish. I wondered what hardships, what success or failure, they had experienced during their expeditions.

"Gene, let's go for water." It was Vincente.

"Sure," I answered.

We picked up a bucket and several canteens, and headed down to the glacier. It was a few hundred yards down to the cloudy streams issuing from the broken seracs and glacial moraine. I was surprised at the number of mule bones scattered about; I pocketed a large bleached vertebra as a souvenir.

After we returned with the water, Vincente led me over to a large rock where he pointed to an inscription scratched into the surface in Greek letters. He had placed it there sixteen years ago when he climbed the mountain.

"¿Que dice?—What's it say?" I asked.

He paused for a few seconds.

"God is all," he answered.

That night the ten of us sat in the candle-lit shelter hut eating portions of a large stew prepared by the two women. I was thinking that I had never found mountaineering easier, when the silence was broken by a pounding on the door. In a second all eyes had examined one another and were now directed toward the door. Bill lifted the crossbar and the doors swung open. A down-coated figure crawled in and lay panting on the floor. As he pulled himself to a sitting position we realized it was Father Fernando de la Mora, the Mexican priest, leader of the Mexican expedition we had encountered at Puente del Inca. He possessed the haunted look common to men who have just completed a difficult climb. Questions were anxiously fired at him from all corners of our dimly lit sanctuary.

"Where are your companions?"

"Are they safe?"

"Did you reach the summit?"

"Did the Polish route go?"

"Are you all right?"

The padre sat down on the floor with the rest of us, pulled himself into a corner, and quietly collected himself before beginning his story.

The candlelight flickered, periodically illuminating his bold, dark features. He began his story in a deep deliberate voice of perfect English. Their planned route on the north side took them up a huge, broken glacier, climbed only once before by a Polish team.

Coco, Vincente's sister, handed him a cup of hot tea. Some of the steam condensed on his eyebrows as he lifted the cup with both hands. He continued.

He explained that his comrades were not strong enough to climb this route. They had finally given up and traversed over to the conventional route, completing the ascent to the summit. However, on their descent they had become bogged down by cold and exhaustion. Fortunately they had reached the shelter hut, Refugio de Plantamura, at about eighteen thousand feet. He had left his two comrades safe in the hut.

We questioned him about his leaving them up there, but he assured us that they would descend without difficulty in the morning. We hoped he was right, but felt somewhat uneasy.

Coco ladled some stew into a bowl for the padre, we refilled our teacups, and the wind lightly pummeled the roof and walls.

In the morning we found an inch or two of fresh snow covering the windblown rock. We had decided to spend a few days acclimatizing and investigating our route, so it didn't bother us.

Dick and I volunteered to travel out onto the glacier in order to secure a better look at the West Face. After breakfast we started off. After three hours we had moved far enough away from the base of the face in order to obtain a realistic view of what might "go" and what wouldn't. We sketched some maps using binoculars for accuracy. We then spent some time circling higher to one side, but finding that our view was unimproved, we returned to base camp.

Upon arriving we were surprised and somewhat uneasy to discover the other two Mexicans had not yet descended. We took off our packs and sat down with our backs against the hut. Bill and Paul squatted in front of us.

"What do you think about the route?" Paul asked.

"I don't know, Paul. From out where we were nothing looks good all the way up."

Dick added, "Everything goes for a while, but ends up in a cliff or shrund or avalanche slope."

Bill looked up at the massif. "We're just going to have to go up there and try some of them."

"At that altitude we're not going to feel like trying very many of them," I said, "Frankly, with our gear and food I still lean toward the conventional route."

"Likewise," said Dick.

"Ralph feels the same way," I added.

"Hell, it's a dog route," Paul said. "Vincente's been up it already."

"Then how come thirty-two climbers have been killed on it?" Dick asked.

No one spoke for a few seconds.

"There have been dozens of expeditions up the dog route," Paul said.

"With all these expeditions, how come nobody has been up the West Face?" I asked.

"No imagination," answered Bill.

"Maybe too much," I answered.

We discussed the problem at some length, and finally came to a compromise. We would attempt the West Face but stay close enough to the north edge so that we could travel over to the "ruta normal," the conventional route, if the going got too tough.

As evening approached Dick and I were stretched out in his two-man tent making the daily notations in our log books, when we heard a voice outside.

"Gene, Dick," it was Ralph's anxious voice, "the two Mexicans are in trouble on a slope high above our camp."

I dropped my pencil and rolled over onto my back.

"What kind of trouble?"

"Frostbite and exhaustion."

As I emerged from the tent, Paul and Bill were standing in the trail with their packs already on, Ralph was hoisting his onto his shoulders.

Paul spoke. "The padre and Vincente were taking a walk and they spotted them trying to come down. The padre is up there with them now. I don't think we'll need any more help getting them down."

"I'll get things ready here," I answered.

As they left I entered the hut and began filling a large pan with water. I placed it on the stove and sat outside waiting.

About thirty minutes later the Mexicans staggered into camp, leaning heavily on their rescuers. They sat down in the dirt, their dark skins cracked around their lips. They were drenched with the haunted look. I spoke to them in my meager Spanish, but there was little enthusiasm. They were both suffering from severe exhaustion and dehydration. I removed their boots. One of them was suffering from moderate frostbite of the toes. I submerged his feet in the warm water.

Afterward I gave them a sedative and helped them into sleeping bags for a prolonged sleep. In a day or two we expected a mule caravan which could carry them out.

That night most of us gathered in the cooking hut for the

customary supper at 10 p.m. A truly international group, I thought as I looked around—American, Argentine, Chilean, and Mexican. We conversed in a complete hodgepodge of languages. I knew English and Spanish. Ralph knew English and a little French. Bill knew English, Spanish, and French. The padre knew English and Spanish. Vincente knew English, Spanish, French, and Italian. Vincente's sister knew Spanish and Italian. Her librarian friend knew English and Spanish. Most of the others knew only their native tongue. Although often feeling an enormous frustration in communication, we quickly perceived that human relationships have a much deeper basis than language. We began singing our native folk songs. The padre had a keen sense of humor and a clear, bold singing voice. He quickly became the song leader. Long into the night candles flickered and the warmth of singing radiated from the small hut high on the hemisphere.

12 ▲
Reconnaissance

THE DAY OF departure from Plaza de Mulas was upon us. It was not necessary to get an early start, since we planned only to reach the access into an unknown valley at about 16,500 feet. We would need at least one day of reconnaissance from that point.

The day before Ralph, Dick, and I had traveled up to about 15,500 feet, gaining route information. We had left a cache of food at that altitude in order to lighten our loads on the first day out of base camp.

While gathering our equipment and supplies together, our gazes often drifted to the steep unclimbed route up this gigantic pattern of ice and rock. It was as if it kept demanding our attention. We had divided our loads into six equal piles. Each of us now prepared to choose a pile to carry. We all made our choice with mixed emotions. You want to pick a convenient load to carry, yet always feel guilty if a remaining load looks more cumbersome. We picked, telling each other we could switch things around later if necessary.

Vincente motioned me over. Like most mountaineers the world over, he was embarrassed to complain of physical problems, not wanting to seem like a weak link. Two things were worrying him. His expected insulated boots had not reached him before his departure from Mendoza, and his present footwear seemed inadequate. Also, he was concerned about his left ring finger, having undergone recent surgery for a tendon injury. The finger could not be straightened, and there was a fragile looking pink scar running its entire length. He was afraid it might break open under stress.

Arrangements were made to borrow one of the frostbitten Mexican's boots. I could not reassure him about the finger. It could easily be torn open. Nothing could be done except to carefully guard it against injury.

The six of us lined up for a group picture with much nervous laughter. It was then that Vincente made the remark I knew was coming—almost always someone compulsively makes such a comment before a dangerous climb: "Smile pretty, this may be our last picture."

Father Fernando de la Mora warmly blessed us and wished us "joyous success." We grunted our packs onto our backs and headed over the avalanche rubble toward a steep icy couloir. The dog cheerfully accompanied us until the terrain steepened; then he sat down and watched us disappear among the rocks and swirls of snow. Lightning flashed across the sky.

We kicked and sometimes chopped steps back and forth across the steep snow gully. The shelter hut below us grew smaller and smaller, ultimately vanishing from view.

A light snowfall patterned our packs and clothing, sending an occasional chilly barrage of snowflakes down our necks.

After several hours we reached the cache of supplies Ralph, Dick, and I had stashed the previous day. We stopped to take off our packs and have some food and water. I smiled as I thought of that scouting trip. After pushing a route through the rocky cliffs, Ralph and I had stopped to rest on a narrow ridge with our packs off, waiting for Dick to ascend. As he climbed onto the ridge, Ralph had moved to one side, toppling his own pack over the edge. We watched as it merrily rolled and bounced down a rocky scree slope for several hundred feet, stopped, then leaped into action again, as if it wasn't going to stop until it returned to base camp. I wanted to laugh, but as the distance grew farther and farther, it became such a disheartening sight that the impulse left me. I wished him a bon voyage as he mumbled down after it.

By the time we were approaching 16,500 feet, there was little energy left in any of us. Bill suggested we dig a camp into the steep snow where we stood. I agreed. Dick said it was the worst campsite he had ever seen. Again I agreed, but nothing within a reasonable distance up or down appeared to be much of an improvement. Dick insisted that he could see a better area about two hundred yards to the west. We suggested he check it out, assuring him that we would follow if it really were better.

He was about half way there when I put my pack back on. "Let's go," I said. "You know damn well that by the time he gets there, it's going to look good, no matter what it is."

We were surprised to find that it actually was a remarkably decent campsite. Dick made sure that no one missed seeing his self-satisfied grin.

Vincente had been lagging behind during the last couple of hours of the climb. We sat waiting for him now, as he completed the traverse over to the campsite. His pace grew slower and finally, within two hundred feet of us, he plopped into the snow gasping. He could go no farther. Ralph and Bill walked over to him. One carried his pack while the other assisted him into camp. His exhaustion worried me.

Bill and I prepared supper. No one was hungry, but we all forced down a meager amount of supper. A few minutes later Paul crawled out of his tent to vomit.

Dick, Vincente, and I lay snuggled closely together in the two-man tent which was to have been the emergency tent. Well, maybe the cramped quarters will help keep me warm, I thought, as I reflected on my complete lack of down clothing. Two sweaters, a wind parka, and ski mittens—some expedition gear! Fortunately, Ralph had carried his down parka with him. Bill had been able to borrow an extra down parka. I was glad I had insisted that Dick take it; he was going to need a measure of comfort, what with this being his first expedition.

It amused me as I thought of the sleeping bags we had used

on McKinley. We had ordered them without zippers to prevent heat loss through the metal. The borrowed bag I was using now had snaps down the entire side, and I rolled over a bit to seal the gaps against Dick's bag.

God, I wished we had our butane stoves. In my mind's eye I could see the small flickering flame of our "weekend trip" gas stove falter and fade.

A cold wet drop pelted me on the forehead. I focused my attention on the tent. Snowy crystals were condensing on the cold surface. Every movement of the tent showered us with a minute snowstorm. Oh, for our double-walled tent, I thought.

As I fell asleep it occurred to me that this time we were challenging a giant with a slingshot.

13 ▲
Into Unknown Valley

As THE SUN cleared the top of the eastern peaks, an explosion of sunlight illuminated our tents. We stirred uneasily. Dick was the first to crawl out of the tent. The clank and rattle of cooking pots was followed by some muffled cursing, and finally the sputtering hiss of the stove. One by one during the next half hour the rest of us crawled out of the tent, speaking little, sitting sleepy-eyed, shivering a bit, awaiting wakefulness.

Vincente sat quietly. The night's sleep had not cleared his enormous exhaustion from yesterday, but his respected gentleness was unaltered.

Paul looked drawn and tired. I wondered if he was in pain. He slowly rose from the pack on which he was sitting and headed behind a pile of huge rocks. I knew he still had diarrhea.

Bill was having some difficulty acclimatizing. His appetite was all but gone, and he had barely managed to consume his breakfast between retches.

It was decided that Dick, Ralph, and I would spend the day in a reconnaissance up into the unknown valley, hopefully determining whether or not a route could be established through it.

Unroped we traversed the rocky snow field and began climbing up a pitch of ever-increasing steepness, which hourglassed into a twenty foot vertical ice wall leading into the valley. As the snow hardened to ice, we stopped to rope up and affix crampons. Chopping steps, we slowly advanced upward until we were clinging to the vertical portion of the ice wall. We were at about the eighteen thousand foot level and panting heavily.

"Christ, I wish we had a couple of ice screws," I said.

"Yeah," grunted Dick. He was too occupied chopping hand holds to be interested in talking.

I thought of the added prestige we had talked about in doing this class of climbing without hardware. "Big deal," I muttered, "I'd trade it all for one ice screw."

"That's it," Dick said. "I've had it. You take it."

"O.K.," I answered, and began the tricky job of trading positions.

We were rising vertically up a corner of the chute, and occasionally I would expose rock while chopping holds. As the time and ice chips flew by, I could feel my energy going with them.

"Ralph," I called down, "how about a shift? I think you can push us over the top in about half an hour."

"Sure."

I began climbing down.

The ice chips tinkled around me as Ralph cut his way up the wall. After about thirty minutes he pulled himself over the top with an audible grunt. I waited for him to situate himself so he could belay me up.

"Won't be able to give you much of a belay," he shouted. "I'm sitting on a slab of snow-covered ice. Don't slip."

Carefully I followed the hand and toe holds up, scooping them free from ice particles, knowing that a slip would somersault Ralph over the cliff. When I crawled over the top I slammed the point of my ice axe into the glistening surface and hung tight while Ralph moved farther up the slope into softer snow and a good belaying position.

"Belay on," he shouted. I knew he could now hold both Dick and me in the event of a fall. We slowly moved up to him.

"We need a fixed rope here, Ralph."

"Yeah, but where do we anchor it without screws, pitons, or pickets?"

We looked around. The only possibility was a large smooth rock, about the size of a sleeping bear.

We belayed Dick while he tied a large loop around the rock and threw the remainder of the rope over the cliff. Two handicaps were painfully apparent even before we placed the rope. The rock was situated too far up from the cliff, so the fixed rope did not reach to the bottom of the cliff. Also there was a reasonable chance that under the tension of climbing the loop would slide over the top of the smooth rock. It was the best we could do. We continued upward.

Traveling up the valley was easy climbing. Snow conditions were good, and the slopes varied between forty-five and fifty degrees, but now we were being confronted with a new problem. Clouds were filling the valley and visibility was becoming poor. We realized that our mission of spotting a route out of the valley was hopeless. We stopped for some lunch and then continued onward for a few more hours, hoping for some miraculous clearing. It didn't come.

Discouraged, we started down. By the time we had arrived at the top of the ice cliff, clouds were beginning to lift from the valley.

"Look," I said in my most disgusted tone. We sat down in the snow for a conference.

"Why the hell didn't it show some signs of clearing while we were up there?" asked Dick.

"It looks like we've got a chance of seeing something now," added Ralph.

We knew we had to head back up, but decided that it wasn't necessary for all three of us to retrace our route. Since the only hazardous area we had encountered was the ice cliff, we formulated a new plan.

We unroped from Dick, and he began plodding back up the valley. Ralph began climbing down the cliff with me belaying him, advancing along the fixed rope. When he reached the bottom he unroped and headed back to camp. I had decided to wait at the top of the cliff for Dick to return, but as sleepiness and cold overtook me I realized that the decision to send Dick alone up this untrodden valley was a pretty shaky bit of judgment. A hidden crevasse, an avalanche, a slip could perhaps conceal him forever. I stood up with a shiver and began plodding up the valley, following his footprints.

By the time I arrived at our lunch site I knew he had probably started down, since a ragged shawl of shadow was beginning to obscure the ledges and couloirs lacing the sides of the unknown valley. Even now I was quite sure the final traverse into camp would be accomplished in the dark.

"Yo!" I shouted in a falsetto to keep my voice from cracking.

An answering yodel drifted down to me.

Several minutes later he was in sight, plunge-stepping down the hill in great strides.

When he was within shouting distance I asked the pressing question, "Will it go?"

He didn't answer until we were close enough to converse.

"It's hard to tell, but I think so. There's one system of ledges that I'm pretty sure will go, and another area that might if it doesn't."

"Sounds good."

"I hope so."

We headed down. It now appeared that we had at least a fighting chance at the West Face. By darkness we were in camp with the news. It was received with cautious enthusiasm. Paul and Vincente still looked desperately tired. I went to sleep wondering if they would be physically able to cope with the next day's strains.

14 ▲
Three Up, Three Down

The early morning hung heavy with gray clouds. We stirred from our tents, and while Ralph fixed breakfast we began to pack our gear to move up into the unknown valley.

"Gene," Vincente called, almost in a whisper. He was sitting on a rock, somewhat removed from the others. I walked over to him and sat down.

"Yes, Vincente?"

"I think maybe I had better not go."

"Oh?" I was more disappointed than surprised.

"I had great difficulty—very tired getting here. I can still go down safely by myself, but if I go up farther I cannot go down by myself, and I don't want to make it difficult for someone else."

I didn't know what to say. Certainly what he said about traveling alone was true, and I didn't want to encourage him to continue if he couldn't, but it's so easy for a climber to lose his mental drive at altitude, and then spend months wishing someone had urged him on.

"Vincente, I think you will feel better after you get started. At least travel up to the entrance of the unknown valley. If you have to go down then it's not too late. O.K.?"

"Yes."

I gave him five milligrams of Dexedrine to boost his spirits and then resumed packing.

Paul walked out from behind a large pile of rocks and approached me.

"Gene, I don't think I can make it."

This time I was disappointed *and* surprised. Although Paul had been more ill than anyone, I had somehow assumed that his tremendous drive and energy would overcome all obstacles.

"Paul, you can make it." I refused to accept the obvious evidence of how weak he had become.

"I don't think so."

I gave him five milligrams of Dexedrine also, and extracted the same agreement I had gotten from Vincente.

By 1:45 p.m. we were strung out making the traverse toward the valley—Ralph, Dick, and I; then Bill and Vincente; and finally Paul. Paul began to fall farther and farther behind, and finally sat down in the snow.

We waited while Bill went back to talk to him. A short time later Bill approached, slowly shaking his head.

"He's gone as far as he possibly can."

I knew it was true.

"Vincente has agreed to go down with him."

"I don't think there's any problem in their going down together, do you?"

"No, I don't think so."

"How are you feeling, Bill?"

"Only fair."

We had traveled on for perhaps twenty minutes when Vincente's voice reached us from below. "Bill!"

Bill was perhaps a hundred feet below me.

What now, I wondered. I waited. Bill moved down to within shouting range of Vincente, but I couldn't make out their conversation. Bill then started up toward me. I moved down until we were close enough to shout back and forth.

"What's wrong?" I asked.

"Vincente says Paul can't go up or down."

I had no answer.

We looked back and forth at one another. It was obvious that we couldn't leave Paul and Vincente by themselves. Paul was weak and ill to the point of helplessness, and Vincente just sturdy enough to care for himself. If Paul didn't improve by tomorrow, someone would have to go down for help and lead a party back up.

Some bitterly crucial moments passed as we all wondered who would sacrifice their bid for the summit. Months of preparation, expense, and anticipation were sinking down the trail to base camp as if down a drain. Each of us could think of good reasons why someone else should be the one.

Finally Bill broke the uncomfortable silence.

"I'll put up the tent and go down with them in the morning."

"O.K.," I answered, but my casual tone didn't reflect how I felt. I felt greatly relieved, but also guilty. I realized what a sacrifice it would have been to myself, and knew it must be at least as much for Bill. I was sorry and disappointed to see our party fragment this way.

My emotional thoughts were rapidly being replaced by thoughts of what equipment and food Dick, Ralph, and I were carrying. I knew Bill and Paul carried the best tent and stove; food was about evenly distributed. It's well that they have it, I thought. It was beginning to snow. Maybe they won't make it down to base camp tomorrow. We'll make do.

Bill waved good-by as he trudged down the hill; another wave of sadness and guilt swept me.

I proceeded to close the distance between Dick, Ralph, and myself. I told them we were now all alone. In losing Bill and Paul I realized we had lost our two best technical climbers. I didn't mention it to Ralph and Dick. We roped up and continued. Snow was falling in large flakes.

Fatigue forced us to change leads periodically as we slowly ascended, with steep snow changing to ice, ever steepening to the vertical cliff. I was leading when I reached our fixed rope. Now with a heavy pack, I found myself using the fixed rope more than I had hoped necessary. Clinging to the ice and supporting at least part of my weight on the rope, I had visions of it gradually overriding the rock and sending me and my companions plummeting down the mountainside.

A fifteen-minute eternity later I lifted my head over the edge of the cliff. The wind was buffeting snow into my face and several seconds elapsed before I could clearly see whether the rope was safely around the rock. When I did I wondered why it hadn't slid over. Crawling over to it, I braced a hand against the rope to keep it in place, and shouted down to Ralph and Dick that they could use it freely now.

A short time later we sat huddled a safe distance from the cliff, thankful that it was behind us. Our rest was short-lived since the wind-stropped cold was beginning to cut through to us. We shivered violently and again started climbing.

Darkness was racing us to the upper end of the valley. It won by a fair margin. The terrain had grown very steep. We used the last rays of dusk to dig a notch into the slope to erect our tent. With the wind and snow battering us, Ralph and I enlarged the platform and then struggled to tame the thrashing tent while Dick huddled in a precarious corner of the notch attempting to ignite our tiny gas stove. We needed fluid desperately. Our intake had been zero since breakfast. The wind howled at his efforts.

"Give it up, Dick," we shouted from inside the whipping tent.

He didn't require coaxing. He tossed the stove inside and crawled in after it.

As I scrunched down into my sleeping bag the irony of our situation irritated me. The three of us intent on the conventional route were now plastered onto a steep snow patch somewhere above eighteen thousand feet in an unexplored valley. Paul, Bill, and Vincente, intent on a new route, were heading for base camp, and perhaps would attempt the "ruta normal" in a day or two.

ON

TARGET

On Muldrow Glacier looking toward the summit of Mount McKinley, ten miles away.   JON L. HISEY

The Lower Ice Fall was a maze of hidden crevasses.   KENNETH C. CARPENTER

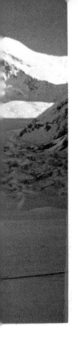

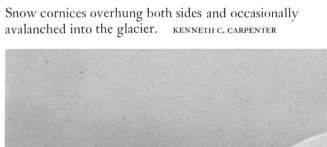

Snow cornices overhung both sides and occasionally
avalanched into the glacier.   KENNETH C. CARPENTER

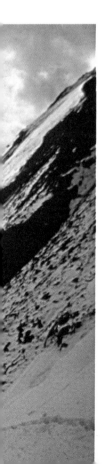

Heading for
Karsten's Ridge
beneath a plume
of driven snow.
KENNETH C. CARPENTER

The formidable
approach to
Browne's
Tower.
JON L. HISEY

The sun which never sets this time of year rests here above Mount Koven and Mount Carpe.

JON L. HISEY

The Aconcagua peak rose out of a dry volcanic wilderness.

T. R. HILL

The highest shelter hut in the world, Refugio de Independencia.　T. R. HILL

Mount Kilimanjaro.　WADE B. CHRISMAN

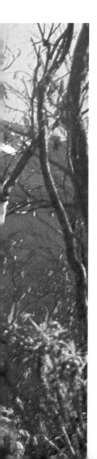

On Kilimanjaro. WADE B. CHRISMAN

On Kilimanjaro.
WADE B. CHRISMAN

My retreat
from
Kilimanjaro.
WADE B. CHRISMAN

15 ▲
Storm

THE BREAKING OF morning found the snowing
largely in abeyance, but the sky was brimming with foul-
looking clouds, boiling in the wind. Dick lethargically began
to dress. I looked at my watch. It took him exactly twenty-
five minutes to get his boots on. He crawled outside to resume
his frustrated project from last night.

Thirty minutes convinced him of the futility. We decided
to risk the hazards of fire in a tiny nylon tent. Several minutes
later found us cramming snow into a pan warmed by a flickering flame. We prepared a stew and luxuriated in the first food
and fluid in twenty-four hours.

We discussed what we hoped to accomplish with the day.
Dick and I would advance up the valley and attempt to pioneer a route out over one of the promising areas he had spotted
during his reconnoiter two days ago. Ralph would shore up
the sagging corner of the tent with snow blocks, melt snow,
and have supper ready for us when we returned. Dick and I
roped up and began climbing.

Something in excess of an hour found us working our way
along a rocky, snow-covered ledge which we hoped would
lead us out of the valley. I was belaying Dick; he was out of
sight when he called.

"Afraid it's a no go."

"How come?"

"Ledge disappears for about twenty feet."

"Isn't there any way to get by it?"

"Not without iron."

Our most hopeful route had been shot down. We back-tracked and headed farther up the valley. I squinted my eyes upward. The snow grew gradually steeper, finally nearing the vertical as it fused with the rocky cliffs surrounding the valley. We proceeded, crunching our crampons into the crusty snow. As the slope steepened, I was becoming increasingly aware of the uncomfortable sensation that a fall could not be arrested by an ice axe. I ignored it and continued climbing. We were heading for a break in the cliff that allowed a zigzag to a tilted plateau encrusted with numerous boulders.

While picking our way across the plateau a mountain storm overtook us. We crouched alongside one of the boulders in an effort to escape the snow-laden blasts, but the wind swirling around its surface drove us to a different rock, where gusts also sought us out. We tried a third, but to no avail. We sat shivering, trying to wait it out. A cold forty-five minutes elapsed.

"Dick," I hollered, almost in his ear in an effort to drown out the wind howl, "we might as well head back."

"We haven't seen if this will go."

I shrugged my shoulders.

He nodded.

We got up and started back. Within fifteen minutes the storm had finished with us and was moving up the mountain. While visibility was still severely hampered, we could at least now see some aspects of the terrain. The plateau became more laden with rocks protruding through the snow, and slowly twisted itself into a steep slope as it disappeared into the clouds like some bizarre, distorted cemetery.

We plodded to the edge of the plateau that dropped a vertical two hundred feet. Peering over the edge we could see part of the unknown valley. At the bottom of the cliff a clear snow slope curved toward the north up the mountain. We decided that it was there we wanted to be. But how to get there?

Dick spotted a small notch at the top of a maze of steep

couloirs and ridges that was not visible from below. He studied them.

"I think I can make out the upper half of a route," he said slowly. "If we can figure out the lower half from below, we might have it made."

"Worth a look," I agreed.

We started down.

About an hour later we were near the point where Dick thought the lower half of the route could be pushed through.

The nibbles of exhaustion and discouragement had turned to large bites. I sat in the snow.

"Let's check it out," Dick said.

"How about tomorrow," I answered.

"I think it would be a good idea to do it now."

Shaking my head I answered, "I don't think I've got it in me. I can just make it nicely back to camp. God knows how long we'd be trying to find a route through that."

Dick began unroping. "I just want a little better look."

"O.K. Don't do anything foolish."

"Right," he answered as he began climbing upward.

"I'll wait here."

He disappeared into the rocks.

About a half hour later he reappeared.

"Will it go?" I asked.

"I think so," he answered, but his lack of enthusiasm left considerable doubt.

Upon reaching camp we found supper almost ready. Ralph had been watching our progress. We discussed the hopes and failures of the day and decided to strike camp in the morning. We went to bed early, with the uneasy expectation of trying to push a route out of the valley.

Deep into the night a snow-laden wind roared over the surface of the mountain, filling in the defects and snow-blasting the irregularities. At about midnight it discovered our tent, a fragile bit of nylon perched on an otherwise smooth slope. The wind tried to free the mountain of this clinging parasite by blowing, buffeting, and then wedging snow between the slope and the tent, forcing the tent out of its niche. Next the wind whirled away the snow support from under the edges of the tent, but the yellow flapping thing still refused to be dislodged.

The battle was well on its way before sleep released us to answer the challenge.

"Hey," Dick said, "I'm being squeezed out of my side."

I popped my head out of my mummy bag for a look. Sure enough, the weight of the snow was crushing in the tent.

"Ralph," I said, "the snow's levering us off the slope."

"I believe it," he answered. His side of the tent floor hung in a sort of a hammock over nowhere.

"We're going to have to dig it out, and keep it fairly clear," I said.

Dick wiggled himself while in his sleeping bag so that he could extend an arm out the drawstring opening at one end of the tent. He began scraping away the packed snow while I loosened it with thumps from the inside.

Taking shifts we cleared most of the snow from the side of the tent. Ralph was struggling to close the zipper on the door end of the tent.

"I can't get the damn thing zipped," he complained as the snow blasted in over us.

"Damn it," he muttered.

"What's wrong?" I asked.

"The damn thing broke."

As the wind layered snow over us, we pulled the tops of our bags around our faces and waited until we would have to clear the tent wall of snow again. It would be about every hour.

Some time later the silence was broken by Dick.

"Aren't you guys worried?"

"Yeah," muttered Ralph, half asleep.

"Sure," I mumbled.

The truth of the matter was that I was damned apprehensive. However, there was little if anything we could do to improve our present situation. I always tried not to worry about the things I couldn't change.

If we were going to be forced into a survival dash, we at least had a fairly decent chance of making it. Except for the ice cliff, there was little technical difficulty between us and base camp at Plaza de Mulas. A good day would be enough if we could stay on route.

The storm continued, making it difficult to detect the beginning of morning.

By noon we had little worth saving in the way of a camp. In spite of our scooping efforts, the snow had collapsed at least a third of the tent. Another third hung over the edge of the slope. The inside was layered with snow whistling through the torn zipper. Our sleeping bags were wet and crusted with ice.

"We have to get out of here while we're still strong enough," I said. "Our morale is beginning to look like this tent."

Ralph and Dick agreed. We decided to travel in the storm. We quickly packed our crusty gear, stuffing the tent without folding it into Dick's pack.

We found the snowy winds easier to face than the diminishing tent. We wound our way upward to the base of the rocky maze that Dick thought would "go."

A few hours later found us jubilantly passing through a steep notch leading us out of unknown valley. Dick had been right.

With the prospect of many daylight hours ahead, we anticipated covering much ground. The fact that we had not consumed food or water since the previous evening was overpowered by our desire to push on.

But the wind was beginning to blow harder and the temperature dropped rapidly.

We pushed on.

Finally we had to face it. We had slowed to a faltering pace and we shook from the cold as we planted foot after foot into the snow. Visibility had become almost zero. The obvious was upon us. We were going to have to set up camp again.

We dropped down about two hundred yards in order to nestle the tent on an almost level spot next to some protective boulders. Setting up the tent was like trying to take a rag away from a large, stubborn dog. The wind lashed hungrily at us.

We crawled into the loudly vibrating tent and into our ice-encrusted sleeping bags. It was 5:30 p.m. We had gained only five hundred feet in altitude. Darkness was soon upon us.

The night dragged on.

Above the noise of the wind and tent came a guttural cry.

"Dick, wake up, you're having a nightmare," I said, nudging him through the layers of sleeping bags.

His cry turned to a mutter which faded off.

Twice more during the night, Dick shouted out during dreams. I wondered if his nightmares were more miserable than reality.

16 ▲
On the Ruta Normal

MORNING LIGHT FILTERED through the torn zipper which I had repaired with safety pins. We stirred almost simultaneously with the realization that the tent was almost quiet.

"The storm's passed," Ralph said, rubbing his sleep-filled eyes.

Dick sat up and began stirring around the gear in the end of the tent, looking for the stove. We had consumed nothing in two days.

After much tinkering the stove was going, and snow melting. A bowl of soup elevated our spirits. We packed our equipment and once more moved out.

High above us a great black bird flexed its gnarled, stringy muscles, propelling it even higher into the endless dark sky, now lit faintly with the morning glow. The condor had spent much time and strength in gaining this altitude of twenty-five thousand feet. At last he could spread that heavily feathered, ten foot wingspan and glide with the windy currents and upsurges. Impelled by hunger, his black eyes searched the Andean high country for movement. Massive talons closed spasmodically several times as if testing their ripping power.

Several hours later we saw a strange object protruding from the snow. It was the bleached bone of a mule haunch.

"We must be close to intersecting the conventional or ruta normal," I said.

"I didn't know mules went this high," Ralph said.

"They brought a group up to 19,700 feet when they built the refuge hut many, many years ago," I explained.

Hours passed.

The rope slackened. I looked up the slope. Dick slowly turned his head as if it were a great effort, and looked down at me. He had completed his two hundred steps of route-kicking. Moving to one side, he sat into the snow, bracing himself with his ice axe between his knees. I continued plodding along in his steps until I reached his level. We laboriously changed rope positions.

"How high?" Ralph shouted from below us.

Dick dug deeply into a pocket and pulled out his altimeter. He held it close to his face, squinting at the dial.

"Nineteen-five."

"Getting thin," I muttered, as I kicked a step into the snow, and counted "one" to myself. "Two, three, and four" followed, "Fifty" made me notice how heavy my feet had gotten. "One hundred" was exhaled through clenched teeth. "One hundred fifty-one." At "two hundred" I sat heavily into the snow, my vision blurred and my consciousness hazy. Several minutes elapsed before I again came completely in touch with cold, blowing reality. We had almost reached the top of a ridge, which was beginning to level.

Dick, and then several minutes later, Ralph dropped panting into the snow beside me. We huddled together, hoarsely communicating between blasts of wind. We agreed that the highest shelter hut in the world, Refugio de Independencia, must be close by. Ralph and Dick took off their packs and slowly, step by step, erased the hundred feet to the top of the ridge. Perhaps twenty minutes passed before I heard a windblown shout.

"We found it."

I stood up and began climbing in the direction of the shout. In a few minutes Ralph and Dick passed me on the way down to retrieve their packs. On top of the ridge I too could see the hut situated in a shallow valley below us. The problems with our inadequate, torn, wet tent are over, I thought. Now we'll have some real shelter before our summit assault tomorrow. I knew from descriptions that the hut was large enough to accommodate three or four sleeping adults.

As we approached, our feelings of elation were turned to despair. A three foot square hole in the roof gaped impotently at us. The entrance doors were torn off and the wind whistled eerily through the defects. The interior was packed with two feet of snow. It appeared to be in worse shape than our tent. This disappointment superimposed on my cold and fatigue had dealt a crushing blow to my morale. I sat shivering violently in the creaking structure as the three of us tried to evacuate some of the snow and prop the broken doors against the doorway. We completed our exhaustion with these projects, finally giving up, deciding to sleep in and on the snow in the hut. Realizing the necessity of food, we ultimately got our stove going, only to have it burst into flames as our stew was cooking. Putting out the fire with snow, we spilled most of our stew. We solemnly divided the remainder and crawled into our sleeping bags.

I had been acutely aware of my aching, icy toes for the last few hours, but now the sensation yielded to a terrifying numbness. I knew I must be nearing the point of no return. As I crawled into my matted, ice-encrusted sleeping bag, I tried desperately to move my toes and bring some circulation back into my feet—but to no avail. After ten or fifteen minutes of this useless activity I nudged Dick next to me. He awakened with a grunt.

"Dick, I'm damn worried, I'm afraid my feet are freezing. Could I warm them in your bag?" I began to realize it wasn't just my feet. My three sweaters were not preventing me from freezing. I knew that when the human body begins to freeze, a severe constriction of the blood vessels in the limbs occurs, in order to sacrifice them to save the body.

"Sure," he answered. He zipped open the side of his bag. I awkwardly twisted my feet out of my bag and placed them in his. But I was unable to feel the warmth of his bag. My feet remained numb. I had gone past the point of no return. After ten or fifteen minutes I returned them to my own bag, and shiveringly attempted to resign myself to my plight. I shook violently all night.

17 ▲
Tragedy

"Help!" the shout barely reached the tiny tents clustered at Plaza de Mulas several hundred feet below, but in one of them Paul stirred uneasily in his sleep as if he had been prodded. Three days had passed since Vincente and Bill had helped him down to base camp at 13,500 feet, and he felt remarkably strong now.

"Help me!" Paul opened his eyes and listened. Was it the wind or his imagination?

"Help! Come help me." Paul heard it distinctly this time. Sitting up in his sleeping bag, he shook Bill.

Paul and Bill tumbled out of the tent and gazed upward at the rocky cliff rising before them. Several seconds elapsed before they spotted a dot of blue near the top of the cliff.

"Who is it?" asked Bill.

"I don't know, but I don't think it's one of our party. Wake Vincente, I'll get the ropes together."

In a few minutes Paul, Bill, and Vincente were plodding upward toward the unidentified climber, moving as fast as the altitude and terrain would allow.

Nearly an hour elapsed before they recognized the lone figure as Rudi, one of two German climbers they had met at base camp after our party had split. The Germans had been climbing throughout the Andes, and had departed Plaza de Mulas several days before with Father Fernando de la Mora in an effort to conquer Aconcagua.

Rudi's gaunt appearance and blank stare reflected the horror he had known during the preceding days. In a final retreat from the miseries of reality he had become almost flippant. He smiled and waved gaily.

"How are your feet?" Bill asked.

"I-don't-know, what-do-you-think?" he answered in that peculiar staccato of people speaking a language that is not their own. He lifted a foot for them to see.

They could hardly believe their eyes. A fringe of ragged stocking covered the top of his feet like a pair of comical spats. The bottom of his dirty, blood-crusted feet ended with a row of blackened toes.

Bill winced but said nothing.

Through cracked, chapped lips, Rudi related a somewhat confused tale of exhausting horror, pausing frequently for sips of water.

"The padre, Dieter, and I ran into a storm near six thousand meters. The padre said to go on. We went. The storm got worse. Still we went on. The storm got even worse, but still we kept going. Then the padre got sick. He couldn't see. He talked like a child. Dieter and I tried to get him back down to Refugio. Finally he couldn't go on any more. He lay down. We tried to get him into a sleeping bag. We couldn't. We lay the bag over him. We took off our boots and got in the sleeping bags. We lay there close together for a long time. Dieter was heavy on me. I told him and he moved away. I don't know where. More time passed. I was terribly cold and I knew I was going to die unless I could get down. My feet were swollen, my boots were frozen, and I couldn't get the boots on. But I knew I had to get down or I'd die. So I went without the boots."

He didn't seem to know if he had spent a night out since leaving them or not. He thought the padre was still alive when he left him, but he wasn't sure. He didn't know where Dieter was.

Bill took off his own double Eiger boots and gave Rudi the inner boots for the trip down.

Bill and Paul had one common thought during the descent—

had the storm cut down our party too? They felt we were at least one day overdue. It was time to organize some sort of a search, both for Dieter and the priest, and for us.

Two hours elapsed before they arrived at the final long scree slope leading into Plaza de Mulas. Rudi hobbled between Paul and Vincente. They led him into the cooking hut, took off the now blood-soaked boots, and gently helped him into a sleeping bag.

Bill, Paul, and Vincente gathered outside the hut. Their looks were grave. How do three men mount a search and rescue on the largest mountain in the hemisphere? How could they also get Rudi to civilization for much-needed medical care? They talked little; precious time was being wasted. Bill wearily dragged his pack onto his shoulders and started off for the Argentine army outpost at Puente del Inca. He would have to travel twenty-seven miles of rugged, rock-churned earth, crisscrossed by the Horcones River. He silently raised an arm as he passed out of sight over the first snow-covered knoll. He didn't look back.

Paul wanted desperately to start up the mountain in search, but he well realized the danger and futility of a one-man effort. He sat outside the hut as a disturbing restlessness settled about him with the dusk.

Suddenly he heard something; he turned his head, stopped, turned again, trying to better pick up the sound. It was the unmistakable clip-clop of hooves. As he stood up, Vincente stepped out of the hut. Appearing over the snow-covered knoll were two figures on mules. Two more mules followed them, heavily laden with supplies.

"Borde Patulla," one of the approaching men shouted. Vincente and Paul ran to greet them.

They conversed in Spanish with Vincente, explaining that they were on a routine border patrol which customarily stopped at Plaza de Mulas. Vincente related the recent happenings to them, and then translated for Paul.

It was agreed that they would leave at daybreak in search

of the padre, the other German, and our group, but they felt that perhaps Paul was still too weak to make the trip. Paul argued in his best legal fashion that he was physically able to participate in the search, and that really they should leave immediately. However, he found that the language barrier screened out all but a few ineffectual words. In utter frustration he retired to his tent.

Before dawn broke, Paul picked up his pack and ice axe and started up the mountain. He had decided that action bore a message in any language. In two hours the border patrol caught up to him and offered him a mule. He accepted with the grace of an attorney winning his case.

18 ▲
Hallucinations Again

A WINDY, CLOUDY morning peered at us through the hole. A few inches of snow covered us.

I had been able to reach a conclusion during the night. As Dick and Ralph awakened and began shaking off the snow, I announced my decision.

"Ralph, Dick, my feet are in bad shape. I expect to lose toes. I'd give almost anything for a ride off this damn mountain right now but that's impossible, of course. So, I've got about seven thousand feet to climb down and probably lose toes or I can climb up three thousand feet to the summit, and then go down. I don't know that the extra three thousand feet will make any difference, but I do know that if I'm going to lose toes, I'll be a hell of a lot happier if I gain the summit first."

Ralph sat up and looked out through the hole.

"Weather doesn't look very good. Maybe if we wait . . ."

"Negative," I interrupted. "I'm going to have to go up or down. We can't wait it out. Right now my toes are numb and I can still climb, but before too many hours the pain will start, and you guys might end up with an invalid on your hands."

Dick sat up for a look out the hole.

"It looks like it might be clearing toward the north. Let's get the stove going and consume as much food and water as possible before we leave."

We agreed that this was a good idea. Dick got the coughing, sputtering stove into its feeble action. Like the stove, human efficiency is not exactly at its keenest near twenty thousand feet. It was almost 2:30 p.m. before we started toward the summit. Ralph carried a pack for the three of us, containing only our flashlights and some candy bars. Dick carried the rope and his camera. I traveled unburdened. The numbness had extended halfway up both feet but did not seem to seriously impede my walking.

We quickly discovered the classical route toward the summit and breathlessly plodded upward. Fortunately, the route was without technical difficulty, not even requiring ropes, but the altitude grew more and more burdensome as we progressed.

During one of our rests I suggested that the three of us walk onto the summit together. We agreed.

Five hours of panting progress brought us to the foot of a large, rocky couloir leading to the summit ridge. We rested more than we moved, glassy-eyed, stumbling and slipping on the rocks. Ten or twelve labored breaths were required for each step forward. Everything ached but my silent toes.

About halfway up the couloir we began to separate, each picking his own route at his own pace. I headed directly for what I thought to be the north summit. Dick climbed toward the ridge between the north and south summits. Ralph wandered between us.

We were advancing about a hundred yards an hour. Some summit dash! The gain from many a step was lost by a foot sliding on the loose rocks back to the starting point. An hour passed, and then two. I felt as if I were suspended in time, like the frustrating sensation of trying to run in a dream and being unable to gain any distance.

Dick, about fifty yards to my right, was stepping onto the ridge between the summits. As he did he raised an arm to us. Ralph waved back. I was busy finding hand and foot holds as I slowly climbed over a large rocky outcropping separating me from the summit. Careful, I thought, don't want to fall now. I crawled over the end of the rock and stood up on the summit plateau. It was a triangle with fifty yard sides tilting upward to the north. I experienced a tremendous urge to walk over to the summit, but remembering our agreement I looked back down on Ralph and Dick to check on their progress. Ralph was twenty-five yards behind; Dick about fifty. I walked over to a snow patch and scratched the names of my four children into the surface with my ice axe, reflecting that there was one more than when I etched their names into the top of Mount McKinley.

I found that I was putting off taking a sweeping view below, wanting to savor it to the last. I lifted my head and the Western Hemisphere spread out below me. The sheer south face rose precipitously to the south summit, somewhat below me. I didn't feel as impressed as I thought I should. I was beginning to worry about getting down. The time was almost 9 p.m. and the valleys below were filling with clouds and darkness. A shiver ran over me; it was getting colder. I pulled my parka tighter around my neck. Ralph was crawling over the outcropping of rock. He stood up and walked over to me.

"We made it, Ralph."

We clung to each other for a few seconds and then looked out over the distant valleys.

"Look at the shadow of the mountain," Ralph exclaimed, pointing eastward with his ice axe. A purple peaked shadow rose, perhaps a hundred miles away.

We walked over to the edge of the summit plateau and directed Dick up the easiest way.

"Congratulations, Dick," I offered. He wore a broad smile on his weathered face.

The three of us joined arms and strode onto the summit. Ralph pulled a political poster from his pack, used in the election of Daniel J. Evans to the governorship of Washington, and placed it on the summit. I pulled a small handmade religious flag from my pocket, given to me by the nuns governing Providence Hospital of Everett, and stuck it into the snow. Dick backed a few feet away, raised his camera, and with a click the shutter froze open. He muttered a few words to it and snapped it back into the case.

"Let's go," I shivered; "it'll be dark in a few minutes."

We dug into Ralph's pack for our flashlights and began down. As I half turned for a last look, my thoughts were upon the price the mountain had demanded of so many mountaineers—thirty-two dead. But the number would rise to thirty-four before I reached base camp.

Almost two hours of flashing and groping in the darkness passed as we gradually descended. We spoke little. Dick interrupted the silence.

"Gene," he began slowly, "I want to ask you something." He seemed almost embarrassed.

"Yes?"

"Where are we, and what are we doing? I seem to have forgotten."

I quietly explained that we had just climbed Aconcagua and were on our way down. I was not alarmed, but I realized he was beginning to lose touch with reality. The altitude, combined with exhaustion and dehydration was beginning to have a familiar effect.

"Are there three of us here or four? I have the feeling there are four of us."

"No, Dick, just three of us." He seemed to accept my answers without question.

We continued our descent, planning to sleep in the shelter hut at 19,700 feet. As we progressed the moon began to rise, silhouetting the irregular rocks projecting from the mountainside. The light reflected off the snow almost made the flashlights unnecessary.

Dick spoke. With a wave of his ice axe he pointed at several columns of protruding rock.

"Gene, I have the feeling that those statues are alive."

"Uh-huh," I answered. We had lost our tracks before the moon came out, and I was trying to again pick up the trail.

I knew we must be fairly close to the refuge. Suddenly I spotted our tracks crossing the snow about a hundred yards below us. Starting down in that direction, I called to Ralph and Dick. They ignored me and began climbing up to the rim of a valley.

"It's up here," they shouted.

"I'm on the tracks," I countered.

They continued upward.

I quickened my pace down the tracks, knowing the refuge would come into view over the ridge. I didn't want Ralph and Dick to get out of earshot.

As I cleared the edge of the ridge, there it was, about two hundred yards down the valley.

"Here it is," I shouted.

"Where?" Dick's voice traveled down from above. He and Ralph were out of sight.

"I'm standing right next to it," I lied, afraid they would continue climbing away unless I was definite.

Dick shouted the news ahead to Ralph.

"Gene's found the hut. Two men in white robes led him to it. I can see them with him now."

19 ▲
THE PRICE OF VICTORY

THE NEXT MORNING seemed saturated with a certain indifference. We were experiencing the usual letdown after our success. We were loggy and unable to clear camp until 9 a.m. Dick seemed recovered from his hallucinations of the previous night. The descent was begun down the "ruta normal," each of us seeking his own speed and direction, eventually being separated by a hundred yards or more as we stumbled down the scree slopes.

After a few hours we were spread by perhaps ten minutes. I was moving unbelievably slowly. My pack seemed much heavier than usual. The dehydration and lack of food over the last week were catching up with me. I plodded along about one third of a mile behind the others.

Dick was within five hundred feet of the Refugio de Plantamura, the hut at eighteen thousand feet, when suddenly he stopped short in his tracks. Stretched out in the trail before him was Father Fernando de la Mora.

"Good morning," Dick announced.

There was no answer, just a swirl of snow that rose from the edge of the body and dissipated into the wind.

Dick advanced. Leaning over, he placed two fingers on the neck, attempting to detect a carotid pulse. There was only an icy stillness.

In Fernando's right hand was an ice axe; a sleeping bag and a small tarpaulin lay beside him. Various pieces of equipment were scattered about him—a stove, a rucksack, two ice axes, a pair of boots. *A pair of boots?*—thought Dick. Where on earth did they come from? The padre still wore his.

Dick took several photographs of the body and the surrounding area. There was no apparent reason for the death. The terrain was without hazard. Shocked and puzzled, he moved down to the refuge hut and plopped himself down against the weathered wooden door. He squinted up the hill awaiting our arrival. Dick was still a little foggy from yesterday, and as the image of the dead priest reappeared in his mind with the snow drifted up against the body, he wondered how he could have thought him alive when he first came upon him. He fired up the stove in order to prepare some hot soup. Ralph joined him about five minutes later.

Another ten minutes elapsed before I joined them. My route had missed the dead priest by fifty yards. Dick told of finding Father de la Mora, and of the extra boots and ice axes. We sat drinking our soup, pondering the mysterious tragedy of the fallen priest, so close to shelter. We talked of his boundless enthusiasm and faith. We had the feeling that death was moving among us. We wondered why he had been struck down, rather than us.

Several miles below us, a column of mounted Argentine mountain troops, alerted as a result of Bill Dougall's twenty-seven-mile march to their post, were moving up as a search and rescue unit. They had sealed off the entire Horcones Valley to restrict the curious.

A mile below us, Paul, Vincente, and the two border patrolmen were scanning the mountainside for signs of the living.

"There's someone," shouted Paul, pointing upward to the moving dots working their way down the rock-strewn hillside.

"Three," added Vincente.

My fatigue had faded with the injection of excitement at seeing the figures and mules down below. With restored energy we rapidly eliminated the distance between us.

It was a greeting of long lost brothers. We laughed and

embraced one another for several seconds before we told of finding Fernando. Paul told us of Rudi's feet, and of Dieter still missing on the mountain. As somber feelings overcame our enthusiasm, we carefully told the border patrolmen where we had found Fernando's body. They goaded their mules up the hill. The rest of us headed downward.

The remaining miles into base camp seemed endless as fatigue overwhelmed us. About a half mile from base camp we were met by a group of young Argentine students who warmly congratulated us and insisted on carrying our packs.

Base camp at Plaza de Mulas had turned into a virtual "tent city." Besides a unit of the army, there were tourists, reporters, and hikers who, hearing of the tragedy, had hired mules to get closer to the scene. Most of them didn't speak English. We sat around somewhat dulled by our exhaustion. My lips were puffy and cracked from the sun. I had no feeling in the toes of either swollen foot, the numbness extending well up into the feet. I looked at my fingertips. They were numb like the toes. The nails were pulled away from the nailbeds at the ends of the fingers. There was no pain. I was worried, but I was consoled by the fact that I was almost off the mountain. I fell asleep in the sunshine.

In the late afternoon the army returned from the eighteen thousand foot level with the bodies of Fernando and Dieter. The German had been found protruding from a snow bank a short distance from the priest. The soldiers buried the bodies temporarily in the edge of the glacier to preserve them until we were ready to leave.

As shadows stalked the valley, the army captain creaked open the hut door and crouching under the beams approached me. I was sitting in my sleeping bag, leaning against the timbered wall. His meager English mingled with my meager Spanish to produce a reasonable degree of understanding. I showed him my swollen, bluish toes and he promised mule transportation in the morning.

The sun broke brightly over the edge of the valley, showering it with light. As we roused, the captain explained that there was a limited number of mules. We would go down in two groups. The first group would escort the cadavers and the frostbitten man (which I recognized as myself); then the mules would return for the second group.

The soldiers went down to the glacier edge to retrieve the bodies of Dieter and Fernando. They returned with the corpses tied onto the saddles in riding position. Bodies crouched over, boots in the stirrups, fists clenched, hair wildly touseled, eyes grimly staring—they looked engaged in a deathly race. Paul walked over and pulled a wool cap down over Fernando's face.

I was helped onto a mule, and fell into line behind their bodies. The captain waved his arm and the caravan of seventeen mules began the long walk out.

As time and the sun slowly passed by during the jarring return trip, my mind recalled the happenings of the past weeks—our lost equipment, the train strike, our new route, the three of us storm-blown in an unexplored valley, our success, Dick's hallucinations, and the deaths. If I could have looked into the future I would have seen some interesting, some disquieting aftermaths of our adventure. Our lost equipment would circle Cape Horn, travel to Norway, and ultimately return to Seattle to be used in other expeditions. Bill Dougall, with his usual enthusiasm, would greet us with iced wine at Puente del Inca for a victory toast. He and his family would stay on in Chile for several more months before returning to Seattle. I would suffer considerably from my frostbite, lose some skin and toenails, but eventually recover to climb with Ralph on other trips. Rudi, the surviving German, would spend months in the hospital and finally have most of both feet amputated. Dick Hill would be caught up in a mental turmoil, quite likely related to his hypoxia on Aconcagua, lose his job, and require months to readjust. He would never join an expedition again. Paul Williams would return in three years to reattempt the climb, and be struck down by pulmonary edema, barely surviving.

We were coming out of the Horcones Valley now and I could see a crowd of people, an ambulance, and a hearse waiting at the beginning of the road. I twisted in my saddle for a last look at Aconcagua. My eyes traveled up the awesome, twisting ridges and cliffs. The Great Inca Sentinel of Stone had claimed two more mountaineers.

PART
THREE

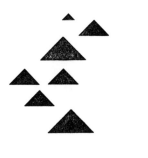

KILIMANJARO

20 ▲
A Little Matter of Directions

The warm, exuberant beauty of East Africa beamed at me through the window as I sat by a small table in the lounge of the Kibo Hotel on the southeast slopes of Mount Kilimanjaro. I was awaiting the arrival of an African guide who was familiar with the northwest regions of the huge mountain, some fifty miles away.

I shifted my blistered feet uncomfortably. I had returned less than twenty-four hours before from a five-day, seventy-mile climb of Mount Kilimanjaro by the conventional route—not a technical climb, but a foot weary, sun-drenched, exhausting experience nevertheless. I looked at my battered felt hat on the table. A garland of mountain flowers circled the brim, placed there as a reward for conquest by the native porters at Mandara Hut. Unfortunately, only four of my party of thirteen had reached Uhuru Point, the 19,340 foot summit of the African continent.

My plans now were to attempt a reconquest of the mountain by a previously unattempted route up the northwest side. I had planned on using the seven most experienced climbers, but four of them had been incapacitated by the brutal malaise and fever of Asian influenza. I was left with Ralph and Wade. It was a pretty thin party. My reverie was broken by the short, shuffling steps of Mrs. Breuhl, a short, chubby, wonderful, overworked, inefficient, motherly little woman. Born in Germany some seventy years ago, and owner-manager of the Kibo Hotel for as long as anyone could remember, she spoke

English and Swahili and somehow made them sound like German.

"Dis ist Ifada," she said.

He stood there with his cap in his hand, somewhat shy, afraid he might not please me. He was a small man with a friendly face and features rather small for a Negro. Wearing an old pair of beat-up mountaineer boots that were meant to be a badge of distinction, he spoke softly. His English was reasonably intelligible, and I soon discovered that he had never been into the area I wanted to enter—but then hardly anyone ever had, so that wasn't much to bother me.

I spread my map out in front of him and asked him if he understood maps.

"No, Bwana," he answered.

"Do you read English?"

"Yes, Bwana."

I opened the small guidebook describing the approach to the area, and pointed to the appropriate paragraph. He shrugged his shoulders. "Cannot read that, Bwana." I began reading to him.

"To reach the start of the Umbwe Route go west from Moshi three miles along the main Arusha road and then turn right. Continue up this road for eight miles, where a signpost points right to Umbwe. Rather than take this track, continue round the mountain for a further two miles and, one hundred yards past a Catholic Mission (on the left), turn right to Kombo Native Market." I stopped reading.

"Do you know the Kombo Market?" I asked.

"Yes, Bwana."

I continued reading. "Turn left in the market and, after fifty yards, cross a bad bridge to the right. After two hundred yards turn right through a coffee *shamba* (native farm). At the end of the shamba (about three hundred yards) turn left toward the mountain and continue uphill to the track junction at the forest guard huts."

I stopped reading and said, "That's as far as we can go by automobile. Do you understand?"

"Yes, Bwana."

"Good, good." I was becoming enthusiastic. I continued with the planned route through the jungle and up the mountain, pointing out the areas on the map, explaining the distances and necessary hours day by day.

After almost a half hour I closed the book, pushed the map away, and asked if he had any questions.

"Yes, Bwana. Do we spend the first night in Mandara Hut?"

I was understandably discouraged. All that explanation, only to find that he didn't even know what side of the mountain I was planning to climb.

"Look," I started, "I need enough porters and food for three men for five days. We'll leave tomorrow morning. Understand?"

"Yes, of course," he smiled broadly. This he understood. I let it go at that.

21 ▲
MOUNTAINEERING BY SAFARI

DAWN SEEMED TO creep up on the jungle. Suddenly the sun erupted over the horizon and began nudging away the shadows. The world seemed full of bird calls, then village bells, and finally people sounds flowing in over our balcony. I stretched luxuriously in my bed with the monkey-fur blanket; I knew it would be my last contact with a bed for something close to a week. My skin was still sore in several spots from the sun and from my boots, but I felt good otherwise, and was filled with the eager anticipation of another adventure. A knock on the door announced the arrival of tea. The maid entered and placed the tray on the nightstand between our beds.

"How do you feel, Ralph?" I asked as I poured our tea.

"Great," he announced.

I knew he was a bit weary, but I also knew he had boundless enthusiasm.

We popped out of bed, showered, and headed downstairs for breakfast and final arrangements. Wade Chrisman was already in the dining room. He had never been on a climb of this magnitude before, but he was a sturdy climber of moderate experience, and his maturity would be an asset. He was an engineer presently employed in the aircraft industry near my home.

He greeted us brightly, but actually we spoke little during breakfast, each of us absorbed in our own thoughts.

It seemed an eternity before we could get our equipment,

porters, and vehicles together in the proper quantities at the same time.

I had found it impossible to rent vehicles. Ultimately the least expensive and practically the only solution was to call a taxi. It seemed absolutely ludicrous to pile our equipment, supplies, and porters into two taxis, and tell the driver, "The mountain please, and hurry."

Luckily the driver spoke good English, and I asked him if he knew the way to Kombo Native Market. He did. We were in luck. The other driver spoke little English, but agreed to follow.

Ralph, Wade, and I climbed into the taxi with a few porters, and Ifada and the other four porters got into the second taxi. We were finally off.

Our taxis wound down the paved road, leaving the south side of Kilimanjaro to proceed across the high plains to the west slopes. The tree foliage met in an arch overhead. Frequent honks of the horn cleared the road of people carrying things on their heads—eight-foot-long bundles of green hay, large water jugs, baskets, and some of the most unlikely things, like hoes, handbags, and paper sacks. Most of the women wore clean, brightly colored frocks; the men wore torn and patched Western clothes. Friendly waves were common and always returned.

After a few miles we passed out of the forest and began our journey along the plains amid the tall sentinel stalks of sisal and occasional baobab trees. These huge trees with trunks fifteen feet across have little foliage for their size, and the natives believe that they are growing upside down, revealing only their roots sticking into the sky. Beehives swung from some of the trees, while others contained clusters of round nests, sometimes fifty or more, providing a haven for many families of weaver birds.

I had made this journey from Marangu to the post office in Moshi the previous day to pick up a survey map of the summit sector of the mountain, and had returned on the public bus. I smiled as I recalled the experience of seeing only three other whites during the entire morning in Moshi. It was an interesting and a worthwhile experience for someone used to being a member of a majority group to find himself a minority group member. We were approaching Moshi now. We stopped at the road junction toward Arusha and waited for the second cab to catch up.

After a forty-five minute unexplained wait, the second cab chugged up behind us and we proceeded. We had a hunch that they had stopped in Moshi, a rather shabby, dusty little town, to socialize since most of the porters rarely get an opportunity to visit "the big city," and they couldn't resist stopping.

Our journey continued through the sisal plantations, and as we left the plains and gradually drove higher toward the mountain we entered the coffee and banana plantations. The roads progressively deteriorated, our cab limped to one side with a flat tire, and the sun grew hotter and hotter.

After much talk, laughing, arm waving, and minimum efficiency, the tire was changed and we bumped onward over rickety bridges, through the Kombo Native Market, and past the *shambas* or native farms.

Through the red-dusted windshield I could see a small group of buildings on the very edge of the road, which was filled with milling people. The unpainted wooden structures looked like something out of an old Western ghost town, only diminutive in size. The street full of blacks, and occasional goats, slowly opened to receive us, and then closed about us as our vehicle stopped.

"Kifuni?" I asked the driver. He nodded. The taxi behind us was not in sight. We waited.

I looked out the open windows. People were dressed in an interesting hodge-podge of Charley Chaplinesque clothes—pants too long or too short, shirts that didn't fit, clothes ripped or patched with bizarre pieces. The faces were not especially friendly. I felt like a hairy white intruder. They gathered near our vehicle to look at us, being careful not to come too close.

I finally judged the faces to be not so much hostile, as perhaps curious and a little suspicious.

One lanky old black stood on a porch with an old hat and overcoat on. The coat hung open revealing a bare chest and a pair of khaki pants cut off just above the knees. Our eyes met for several seconds before his face broke into a toothy grin.

We got out of the car. The other taxi was not in sight yet. Our driver and a couple of porters started walking back down the road. The rest of our porters wandered off into the village.

A husky young Negro, whose clothes came closer to a fit than most of the others', walked up to me and began talking in Swahili. After thirty seconds I had exhausted my stock of Swahili phrases, and was forced into silence or repetition. Alternately I tried a bit of both. I tried to explain that I didn't speak Swahili, but he continued to talk, and from his intonation I guessed he was questioning me. I tried answering with smiles and mutters, and finally came to the conclusion that he was primarily interested in impressing the gathering group that he was able to communicate with this "Bwana."

The driver returned to announce that the other taxi was stuck, and then departed again with most of the porters.

I wandered a hundred feet down to the end building on the road. Several people clustered about the front of a tiny shop; the hand waving and loud bargaining attracted my interest. Over the half-door I could see a sweating black in a skull cap and undershirt and dangling cigarette with a long ash protruding from his lips. An ancient-looking cast iron scale was perched between him and an arguing woman. On the scale pan were several pieces of hacked meat. He turned toward several hanging strips of fly-covered meat and intestine. With a long narrow knife he sliced off a piece, tossing it onto the scale pan. More argument ensued. I had discovered the local meat market. One of our porters stood in line.

After some time a grinding of wheels and gears finally announced the arrival of the second taxi. Our driver reappeared and we piled into our taxi and proceeded up the road.

As our vehicle twisted and lurched down the rutted road, it became apparent that the road was gradually giving way to a wide grassy path. I looked at the map. We were approaching the forest boundary. We pulled to one side and stopped. In apologetic tones the driver explained that he had better not try to go any farther for fear of ruining his taxi. The second taxi was again out of sight.

We unloaded the vehicle and sat in the grass. The porters produced some sandwiches, hard-boiled eggs, and tea for our lunch. After some minutes our driver decided to take his taxi back down the road and pick up the remaining crew from wherever they were stuck.

"Dammit," muttered Ralph, as he jumped up, swatting and brushing himself. A huge black ant fell off his arm.

"They mean," smiled one of the porters.

Ralph moved away from the spot and squatted over the grass, rather than sitting on it.

Ten minutes elapsed before the taxi arrived full of porters. We mounted the gear on our backs. I took an altitude and compass reading, and headed north up the path, with Ralph, Wade, and seven porters behind.

Two hours brought us to the end of the trail and the beginning of the jungle. Rain had overtaken us, and in spite of our rain gear, parts of us were rather soggy. I verified our position on the map and ducked into the foliage. The wet jungle absorbed our party like a great green sponge. I thrashed along, trying to clear at least a passable way for the porters balancing loads on their heads. Going was slow as we climbed over and under moss-covered logs and beside huge ferns fifteen and twenty feet high. Long vines hung down from the treetops.

Frequently I gazed toward the upper reaches of the treetops where the light filtered through, hoping to spot some monkeys. On the other side of the mountain during our approach to the conventional route, a group had moved into a nearby tree. That night an English member of our party and I had gone out into the forest and had sat quietly for a half hour attempting to spot a leopard, since they frequently stalk monkeys.

A sudden crashing of the underbrush startled me. I rushed forward hoping to catch a glimpse of whatever it was. The terrain was too steep and thick for elephants or giraffes. I missed seeing it. Examining the broken foliage I found deer-like tracks, probably those of a bush-buck. We continued.

Our porters didn't ordinarily sweat much, being accustomed to the climate and the loads, but they were sweating now. I could hear their grunts as they wrestled their loads up the steep jungle-covered mud.

"Stop, Bwana?" came the call from below and behind.

"Yes," I answered, coming upon a fairly level spot.

I settled myself into the damp greenery and slid my pack from my shoulders. One by one the porters appeared through the vines and ferns to pantingly drop their loads.

"Much farther?" one of the glistening black faces asked.

"Not much," I answered. "We rest here."

A quiet settled over the group as they waited for enough energy to begin talking. Wade sat with his back against a giant fern intently digging a tick out of the back of his hand.

After five minutes conversations began, and a few minutes later there were a few smiles and some laughs. Our porters sat in a fairly wide circle, and we sat against some trees off to one side. Two of them began breaking and dropping pieces of wood in the center of their circle, and soon a fire was smoking and crackling. A chill was spreading from our sweat-soaked shirts. We quickly moved into their circle. Others began sharpening two long sticks. The porter I had seen at the meat market pried open an old square metal can of four gallon capacity, and a three foot long strip of beef was withdrawn. There was a horizontal slash every few inches which allowed the meat to be corkscrewed onto the wooden skewer. The meat was covered with white maggots. A few fell off as the meat was forced onto the stick, but most of them clung tenaciously. A second strip was pushed onto the other skewer, and both were thrust over the yellow flames and immediately began sizzling.

I had known that the natives carry ears of corn in their pockets to munch while on the trail, but until now I had not known anything about the rest of their diet.

As the meat was at least partially cooked, pieces were trimmed off and passed to the eager mouths encircling the pile of glowing coals.

With each of the porters receiving several large hunks of meat, I began to wonder if they would offer us any. Considering the lack of even the barest rudiments of sanitation, I had pretty well decided to refuse such an offer when a knife was thrust under my nose with a piece of meat stuck on it. I pulled the piece off and began chewing. Wade and Ralph followed suit. The flavor was good. The maggots were more tender than the meat. We finished our rest, put out the fire, hoisted our loads, and prepared to move on.

As time passed, a growing murmur of mumbles and grumbles, recognizable in any language, was beginning to follow me. Even though I couldn't understand them, the discontent was no mystery. We were traveling through jungle on scarcely anything that could be called a trail, although I occasionally found an ancient blaze on a tree. Not only was the route difficult, but the unknown was even more menacing to these people. Also, their accustomed four hours of porting had been extended to five hours already with no camp in sight.

I was reluctant to stop for fear I wouldn't be able to get the porters moving again. But there was no choice. The sweating, glistening porters deposited their loads with a thud and a grunt, and sprawled onto the wet ground.

"Camp here, Bwana."

"No, not yet." I felt guilty, but we had to keep on schedule, not only because we had to get out on the quoted day to rendezvous with the taxis, but also because we had only a limited supply of food with us.

More mumbling occurred as my words were translated and passed among the porters. Ifada ambled up.

"They want camp here, Bwana."

"I know, but we can't yet. Tell them that a short distance ahead there is a covered shelter."

He told them in crisp, authoritative Swahili.

The mumbling gradually faded.

Wade passed his canteen to the porters. They eagerly drained it. Ralph and I passed ours to the porters also. They drained ours.

After several minutes their cheerfulness began to return, and I used my feeble knowledge of Swahili to make a joke. I looked them over and said, "M-tu, under the M-ti, by the Umbwe." It was a play on the similarity of some of their words. It meant men under the trees by the Umbwe River. They laughed heartily, but I wasn't sure whether it was at the joke or my inept attempt to speak their language. Either way it broke the ice. Several disappeared into the jungle with our empty water bottles and returned with them full.

As we reloaded our packs to move on I hoped to hell that the "shelter" was only a short way off.

A half hour later found me slashing my way up a steep hill expecting the grumbling from behind to start at any moment. As I seized a root and pulled myself up to the top of the muddy ridge, there it was. The guidebook described it as an "all-weather shelter" at the ninety-four hundred foot level, but actually it was only an eight foot square area with posts erected in the corners and several lashed across the ceiling. It was entirely open, but situated near a rocky overhang. The natives seemed satisfied, even joyous, but we were a bit disappointed.

I had trouble believing this was the "all-weather shelter." Considering the possibility that the real shelter was just a little farther off, and wishing to gain some idea as to what the next day's travel would be like, I deposited my pack and told Ralph and Wade that I was going to scout ahead.

After a couple tries that ran smack into cliff, I found a way up and over the rocky bluff. I pushed on rapidly. It became apparent that the ridge was narrowing and the vegetation thinning. With luck I would be able to glimpse the mountain. As I burst through the foliage, a huge rugged cliff of Kilimanjaro thrust itself at me from across several valleys. Pinkish hues flowed from the snowy top, splattering the cliff below.

I looked at my altimeter; I had climbed three hundred vertical feet. Suddenly I realized that dusk was upon me and I was some distance from camp without my pack or flashlight. A dumb move, I reflected. Starting down the ridge, I was almost immediately plunged into darkness. I hadn't traveled very far before I realized I might have considerable difficulty finding my way back. I wasn't as worried as I was disgusted. After a reasonable distance I began shouting. No answer. I listened for voices, but I heard only jungle sounds. The only solution was one of quiet perseverance. I pursued this course, moving quietly, stopping, listening, occasionally shouting. Ultimately I heard voices and quickly stomped into camp. The natives sat humming and chanting around a large fire.

"Get lost?" Ralph chided.

"As Daniel Boone used to say, 'I've never been lost, but I admit to being mighty confused for a few days at a time.'"

"I was just about to go looking for you," Wade commented.

"Actually I sort of got hypnotized by the mountain and caught short by the sunset. It's pretty dark out there."

Ralph passed me his water bottle. "There are swimming things in the water here."

I held the bottle up to the firelight. Several wrigglers periodically bobbed crazily to the surface to breathe.

"They're mosquitoe larvae," I said, rather surprised.

"They won't drink much," consoled Wade.

"It's just a matter of timing," I offered. "You drink when they're down and stop when they're up."

"Thanks for the tips, buddies," answered Ralph as he carefully poured his bottle cap full of water to check it before drinking it down.

After a hot supper cooked by Ifada over the fire, we stretched our tent over the top of the shelter frame and invited the natives to sleep under it with us. However, the limited space allowed only a few to take us up on this offer, and the rest slept under the rocky overhang.

Before I fell asleep, my mind wandered over the problems. We were on schedule so far, but tomorrow was going to be an enormous challenge. I wanted to move the party from ninety-four hundred feet to almost fifteen thousand—the equivalent of two days' travel on the conventional route. I slept lightly.

Dawn stirred us into activity. The hours that followed found us moving out of the moss and fern covered rain forest higher up onto the ridge. The view of the mountain that had confronted me the previous evening was now obscured with fog and clouds. We had used fixed rope up one of the very steep slopes, and had continued to find occasional tree blazes and other signs of previous travel, including some rather antique pitons in a crude shelter at about twelve thousand feet.

It was at this point at 1 p.m. that the porters wanted to stop for the day. I explained to Ifada that we couldn't stop yet, but could take a long break. The porters immediately built a fire, and sitting with them in a circle we again joined them in eating their maggot-infested meat. After an hour and a half we pushed on.

We were now above timber line and the large plants were either purple flowered lobelia, reaching five feet in height or giant groundsels, a striking twenty-foot-tall plant resembling a palm tree trunk but with a huge cabbage on top instead of palm fronds. From a distance they looked like strange quiet people standing amid the rocky terrain.

Another hour's climbing took us to thirteen thousand feet, pretty well above even the groundsel. The only obvious vegetation consisted of an orange-colored moss hanging from the rocks like some unnatural, displaced beard.

Lightning, thunder, and occasional sprinkles of rain had followed us up the ridge. I kept noting the interval between the lightning and thunder, worrying about a shorter interval indicating an approaching storm. The lightning had remained close enough to keep us uncomfortable but not so close as to abort our progress.

Ralph, Wade, and I had outdistanced most of the porters, only a few of whom kept up with our pace. The other five were strung out over the barren rocky wilderness. We began to hear them shouting.

"What do they say?" I asked the porter at my side, knowing he understood some English.

"Go back, go back," he answered.

We sat down among the rocks and drizzle.

"It's not going to work," I said shaking my head. "We'll never be able to coax them up another thousand feet."

"We need another plan," added Wade.

Several seconds elapsed as we each considered the possibilities.

"We could call it quits," I said, more to get Ralph and Wade's reaction than as a solution.

"After all we've been through, I don't think we're to that point yet," Ralph offered.

Wade shifted for a more comfortable spot amid the rocks.

"Maybe if we carried part of their loads we could move them up. Some of those guys have enormous loads."

We nodded our agreement.

"I think we've got three alternatives," I started. "First we could offer to carry part of their loads, and see if we can get them to continue."

"I'm not sure they'll go for it," Ralph added.

"True," I agreed. "Secondly, we can pull the essential stuff out of their loads, send them down lower, and continue on our own. And finally, if neither of those is accepable we've got to quit."

"Let's see if they'll go for solution one," said Wade. "If not, I'm ready for solution two."

"How about you, Ralph?" I asked.

"I agree."

An hour passed before the last porter wearily shuffled among us. Ifada was behind him, in order to see that no one was left behind.

I explained the plan to Ifada. He listened carefully and then said, "They go on," rather matter-of-factly.

"But they're exhausted," I argued.

"They go, they go," he insisted and began haranguing and scolding each man, shaking his small finger in their faces. They began to get up and lift their loads.

"Wait," I interrupted.

Ralph, Wade, and I walked to the heaviest-looking loads and began pulling out pieces of gear, stuffing things into and onto our packs.

We then waved them on, and our expedition again began to serpentine its way upward between the boulders.

By 6:30 p.m. we were approaching the barren rocky overhang at 14,700 feet that we would call our base camp for the next several days. The natives were rather unenthusiastic about the site, but grateful that they could rest the next day.

While we set up our tent, they huddled together shivering under the overhang. It required little time to realize their normal energy was being destroyed by the altitude, the cold, the unknown, and their fatigue. Ralph removed his wind parka and put it on the coldest-looking porter, while Wade and I began constructing a windbreak out of rocks.

Ifada looked over the area and crisply shouted orders to a couple of the more hardy porters. They grimaced and said something in Swahili. He replied with something more stern, and the three of them headed down the valley. I discovered

they were heading down after firewood. Ralph, Wade, and
I decided they didn't have a chance of finding any.

By the time they returned laden with bundles of small
branches, we had finished constructing the windbreak and had
secured several gallons of water from the nearby glacial creek.
A fire was started and spirits slowly crept back into our exhausted crew. After a light supper we slept.

22 ▲
Falling!

"Is time, Bwana."

Ifada extended his arm into the tent, and I sat up in my sleeping bag to receive a pot of tea and three cups. I turned on my flashlight and began pouring the tea.

"What time is it?" Ralph asked.

"One-thirty," grunted Wade as he moved on his side to make room for the steaming tea.

"Bwana." It was Ifada again, this time with milk, sugar, and a small plateful of cookies.

"You want I should go with Bwana?"

"No, Ifada, thank you, but I don't think so."

I didn't quite know how to let him down without offending him. As our "guide" he was trying to fulfill his responsibility. I wondered what he thought our route up the glacier would be like. I had the greatest respect for this strong little mountain man. If he had been properly equipped we would have been tempted to take him with us.

We pulled on our wind clothes and crawled out of the tent. The cool clear air snapped at our nostrils. The full moon streaked the rocky ridges and drenched the mountain with pale light. It was our first good view of the mountain. I spread the map and photograph of the mountain out on the ground and waved Ralph and Wade over with my flashlight.

"There's the Great Breach Wall," I said, pointing at the mountain and then to the map and photograph. "The Little Penck Glacier must be on the other side of that long rocky island." Again I pointed at the mountain, and then the map and photograph. Continuing on the map, I traced the route with my finger.

"We will pass just north of the Shark's Tooth Lava Tower, then up the Little Penck at this point. We may have a problem distinguishing the Little Penck from other glaciers; however, we won't know that until we get over there. Everyone agreed?" They nodded their agreement.

We hoisted our packs on and began our trudge down to the first stream crossing. The edge of the stream was criss-crossed with a brittle layer of thin ice. We stopped to top-up our water bottles, then up to the ridge top and down to the second stream crossing. The Shark's Tooth Lava Tower loomed loftily to our left, eerie in the moonlight. A small light flashed to us from the tower. It was unbelievable, and we soon realized that it must be a small snow patch reflecting the moon.

A slow plod took us up to the top of the next ridge and down to the third stream crossing. We clustered in a level spot to rest for a few minutes. Ralph pulled out a bag of cara-mels and passed them around.

"We should be able to see our glacier when we get to the top of this ridge," I whispered. Ralph and Wade whispered their agreement. Strange how people whisper in the early hours, almost as if they don't want to disturb the stillness.

We got up, and with a deep breath and a stretch, continued up the last scree slope. As we neared the top, my pace quick-ened with the expectant enthusiasm of seeing our route.

"There it is," I announced.

"Doesn't look too tough," Ralph added.

Wade quietly surveyed the potential problems.

We looked far up the mountain to see the wide white rib-bon of glacier flow steeply down the valley, wrinkle and tear among the rocks, and then smooth out for a half mile to end in a fifty foot high ice cliff. My eyes traveled the distance sev-eral times, and then concentrated on the lower portion for the easiest way onto the glacier. There were a few acceptable methods.

Down the scree and across several icy snow fields, we reached the bottom of the valley with the glacial snout towering over us.

I dug my ice axe into the slope and, straddling it for stability, proceeded to strap on my crampons. Ralph and Wade braced themselves similarly and affixed theirs. Uncoiling our rope, I cinched an end to my waist and tossed the remaining coils to Wade.

I looked up the steep icy pitch and slammed a steel-pronged boot into the slope. A stroke or two of the ice axe established another step. Ralph and Wade were still uncoiling rope, but there was no reason to wait for a belay from below since it wouldn't help anyway; a slip would not drop me lower than their level. Another couple dozen chopped steps brought me to the brim of the fifty-foot pitch. I stepped over the lip onto the smooth glacier, established an ice axe belay, and shouted down to Wade. He followed in my steps and then belayed Ralph up.

The next hour was spent moving across the smooth glacier of fifteen degree pitch bringing us to the foot of the ice fall, the broken, twisted part of the white ribbon. We rested for some minutes. The sky was light, but this side of the mountain would not see the sun until well into the afternoon. Clouds were beginning to fill the valleys below us. I shook off a chill and stood up.

"Let's move on."

Carefully I studied the steep pitch ahead. It started as hard-packed snow and turned to ice through most of its steepness. An occasional rock jutted through. Not too bad, I thought. An ice axe belay from below, then the rope over the rocks and I would have a reasonable amount of protection. I picked out a couple of belay spots where I could move Wade up, and led off, carefully chopping toe holds, and occasionally a hand hold for easier balancing.

Ralph and Wade moved smoothly up below me amid the tinkling, bouncing crystals of ice dislodged by my step-cutting. Slowly we zigzagged up the ice, arriving on the forty-five to fifty degree upper glacier which rose thousands of feet in a huge dome above us. The glacial surface was thin crusty snow over the ice. Open crevasses were not evident. We rested in standing position for several minutes before pushing on.

By the time we reached seventeen thousand feet, the altitude was gnawing at our endurance, our enthusiasm, and perhaps the edge of our reason. It was approaching ten o'clock and we were high on the endless dome of glacier, slowly, step by laborious step, climbing skyward. The pitch was at least fifty degrees of solid ice, and a mass of gray churning clouds had covered the slopes and valleys below us.

I stopped for a few extra breaths when I heard Wade call from his spot in the middle of the rope.

"I think we ought to go back, Gene."

I didn't answer, waiting for the forthcoming explanation.

"I don't like the looks of the clouds down there. We're not going to find our way down."

"Do you think the visibility could get any worse?"

He looked down for a few seconds. "No," he replied.

"Then we may as well climb for a few more hours. Our problem finding a route won't be any worse then, and it might be better."

"I've never climbed an ice slope this steep before," he answered.

"You're doing fine."

I plodded upward, slamming my crampons firmly into the slope. But I wasn't satisfied with our progress during the next half hour. Ralph was unable to keep up with the slow, continuous pace I was setting, and required frequent additional rests. He lost his footing several times, and fell into self-arrest with Wade holding him. I stopped to look at my altimeter— 17,200 feet—another few thousand feet to go. It was 10:15 a.m. I shouted down to Ralph and Wade.

"We've got to do better or we're going to run out of time." I paused to breathe. "We'll push on for two more hours, and then decide whether to go for the summit or go for home." As an afterthought I added, "Ice is getting so hard and steep, I'm beginning to have doubts that we could stop ourselves with a self-arrest." I continued the grueling methodical plod, and then it happened.

It was so violent, so quick. I was plummeting down the icy slope. Although I had been yanked over backward, starting the fall head down on my back, I had instinctively brought myself into the head up, face down, ice-axe arrest position. Showers of ice crystals bit into my cheeks and ricocheted ten feet into the air as my axe stuttered over the surface. My mind and body searched for a halt as our speed reached an ever increasing crescendo. The first thought bursting into my mind was that there was a short but less steep pitch about a thousand feet below us. If we were still conscious or alive by then, perhaps we could stop at that point. The second thought was more realistic. With our speed increasing as it was, we would pass that spot in excess of fifty miles an hour, and streak off into space at a point a few hundred feet below where the upper glacier ends.

Wade was yanked over backward also. Hurtling down the slope with his axe chattering on the ice, he automatically worried about losing his glasses, but then realized he might never need them again. While streaking down the glacier with the surface ripping at his clothes, Ralph too realized we weren't going to stop. He wondered if our bodies would ever be found.

In desperation I tried the only thing left to alter our fall. I spread my legs and dug my crampons into the ice. There was no pain, just a gigantic wrench as my body crumpled, bounced, then cartwheeled over the slope past Wade and Ralph, and came to a moaning stop. Ralph's axe had found a hold, stopping Wade and then myself with a rib-cracking jerk. Perhaps my maneuver had helped slow us, but I doubt it. I continued to moan for several seconds, not really knowing why. Then several seconds of intense quiet settled over us.

"Is everybody alive?" I exhaled. Grunts of acknowledgement followed from Ralph and Wade.

"You guys hurt?" I asked. It was several moments before they answered that they seemed to be unhurt. They asked about me. I replied that I wasn't sure about my ankles.

I pulled an ice screw and a carabiner out of the pocket of my pack and anchored our rope to the mountain to prevent another slide. I dug into my pocket for my altimeter—16,900 feet. We had fallen three hundred vertical feet. Taking stock of my condition, I found almost all the buttons had been ripped off my down parka and the heavy zipper had been torn in half. I looked at my ankles. The left crampon had been rotated around to the side of my boot. I took it off and reapplied it properly. Cautiously I atempted to stand. A bolt of pain and weakness stabbed at my left ankle. I tried to put weight on my right one, but got pretty much the same reaction. I was unable to stand. I refused to believe it until I had tried several more times with the same result.

"Ralph, Wade, I can't seem to stand up!"

I wasn't panic-stricken but I was damned concerned. It was going to take us at least the rest of the day to get off the ice, and a forced bivouac on the glacier might be difficult for me to survive in this condition, especially with the foreseeable tough days ahead. And there were still enormous problems after we were off the glacier. Somehow we had to cover the three miles or so back to the tent, and the ten rugged jungle miles out to civilization. We would face them one at a time. Right now the *only* worry was getting off the glacier.

I was anxious to start the descent. I took off my crampons to prevent their snagging on the slope and further injuring my ankles. Breaking several of our trail-marking wands into appropriate lengths, I taped them as splints to my ankles. It seemed like an unnecessarily long time for Ralph and Wade to get organized for the descent. However, fatigue and fear battered their already exhausted frames. Wade had lost some food and equipment in the fall, and had sustained a nasty leg laceration which he didn't discover until the next day.

We planned our descent into the fog. Visibility was almost nonexistent. I suggested Wade lower me feet first using the ice screw as a belay. At the end of the rope I would place another ice screw. Then Wade and Ralph would descend, bringing the upper screw down with them. They began lowering me, and the fog enveloped me like quicksand.

As we slowly moved down, they quickly streamlined the operation in the following manner. Wade would belay me with an ice screw or his ice axe for the 150-foot length of rope. Ralph would travel down alongside the rope, secured to it by a sling rope with a prussic knot. When he reached me at the end of the rope, he would set up a belay and bring Wade down.

We continued this process for hours and hours and hours. Wet, cold, and snow seeped through my clothes as I slid on the ice. I began shivering violently and uncontrollably. Inadvertent twisting of my ankles produced exquisite pain. The pain, cold, and shock were beginning to gnaw at what little morale and spirit I had left. I fought them as best I could, but I knew they were making dangerous inroads.

The idea of going down through the ice fall the way we had come up began weighing heavily on my mind and gradually began to dominate my fears. I was afraid I would slide over one of the icy cliffs. The rope wasn't long enough to reach bottom, and retrieving me from the dangling end would be extremely difficult—probably impossible with the equipment we had. It would mean anchoring the rope with me hanging on the end until they could descend unroped for help and equipment. This would take a minimum of two or three days, and I knew I couldn't survive it.

I tried to remember details of the glacial slopes to the north. They looked far easier and safer in my mind's eye. I explained my fears to Ralph and Wade, and my preference for moving north for our descent. They were both dubious, insisting even a difficult known was better than an unknown. I wouldn't be swayed.

In lowering me, my weight took the shortest distance down.

Consequently the only way I could move laterally on the slope was by crawling with hands and ice axe. I began making my way north with each successive belay. The fog hung on us. We moved for hours in an eerie light as if the world had become stuck between darkness and day.

Finally we arrived at the connection between the upper and lower glaciers. The way we had come up lay several hundred yards to the south. Ralph advanced to scout out the best route down. I pulled myself to kneeling position, resting on my ice axe. My clothes were wet from sliding in the snow and I was cold and miserable.

"How does it look, Ralph?" I asked as he appeared from around a huge rock.

"Not so good. There's a rocky fifteen-foot cliff below us here that drops into a steep snow gully. I can't see more than a hundred feet down it. Up higher to the north it looks very easy."

My morale plummeted. We had not gone far enough north before dropping in altitude. I knew I couldn't climb up and around. I didn't want to swing south to our original route; anyway, that would also mean climbing some distance up and around. The present route sounded treacherous. I was afraid and I hated both the cliff and the feeling of fear, but it had to be done. If I could just make it past the cliff.

"I'll get well-positioned in a good sitting belay and ease you over," Ralph said. His voice was full of confidence.

"Do you think you can hold me with a sitting belay?"

"Sure."

I shook my head dubiously. "Why don't we have Wade put in an ice-axe belay above you just in case you can't hold me?"

"Fine."

The belays were fixed and I crawled over to the edge and peered over. It was exactly as Ralph had described it: a fifteen-foot cliff followed by steep snow. A few large rocks off to one side near the bottom would allow a spot for me to wait for Ralph and Wade to descend.

"Belay on," Ralph shouted.

I pivoted on my stomach and poked my legs into space. The rope grew tight around my waist as I squirmed over the edge, and as it tensed with my weight, established a vicelike grip under the edges of my ribs, at the same time forcing my pack and parka up to cover my neck and face. I dangled, swinging in a circle, painfully. Then I dropped, perhaps only a foot or two, as Wade's ice axe belay picked up the rope slipping past Ralph. I groaned and choked. They lowered me to the snow slope where my ankles, momentarily supporting my weight, shocked me with a new pain before I collapsed to the snow and crawled over to the rocks.

"Belay off," I shouted.

Still gasping, I felt the enormous relief of having survived the most dangerous part of our descent, this cliff and everything above it. If I can only make it off the snow now, I thought.

Nestling down among the rocks, I awaited Wade's and Ralph's climb down the rocky pitch over to the side of the cliff. After a few minutes of silence I heard their belaying signals. Crouching my head against the rocks, I valued their protection, for the air was pierced by the occasional zing of a dislodged stone as one and then the other climbed down to me.

We continued our downward progress of sliding and belaying. The distance down to the snowline seemed much farther than I remembered. My spirit began waning again. I promised myself a reward upon reaching the end of the snow. I would shake the snow out of my clothes, put on my down vest, and eat my last piece of hard candy.

An agonizing duration later, I slid across the last snow field and crawled onto the rocks. Pulling off my pack, I pulled out my down vest, fluffed it up, and took off my snow-encrusted parka. After plunking the piece of candy into my mouth, I took the wand splints off my ankles, and began layering adhesive tape in a figure eight pattern over my boots.

"I think we've descended too low," Wade said, peering squintingly into the fog.

"We should have come down the way we went up," added Ralph.

"I know where we are," I persisted. "The snout of the glacier has got to be there." I pointed south into the fog.

Wade shook his head.

"The snow doesn't go that far into the valley," I argued.

However, we all agreed the base camp was generally south, and we agreed on that direction.

"Why don't you go ahead and get the porters," Ralph suggested. "I'll stay with Gene."

"Wade, I'm going to try and hobble to the Shark's Tooth Lava Tower, or at least in that direction."

"We'll find you."

At that moment the fog suddenly lifted from the south where the glacial snout now towered just above us.

"See," I pointed.

No comment.

Wade moved down the valley. Ralph started out slowly, attempting to find the easiest route for me. I struggled painfully to my feet, and with a short shuffling gait began moving. Although I walked like a hundred-year-old cripple, I was intensely aware that getting off the snow had increased my survival time from days to weeks.

Picking my way along, stumbling frequently, I cursed in frustration rather than despair. Little by little, even at my feeble pace, I began covering some distance. Close to an hour passed torturously by. The pain stabbed at each ankle as I moved forward, slow step by slow step, hunched over and leaning heavily on my ice axe. I knew I could not go much farther. Continually I fixed new goals—just make it to that pointed rock, now just to the notched boulder over there. With each goal I reached I set the next one nearer and nearer, but it seemed to take longer and longer. I lurched out of balance and fell to the ground with a jarring grimace. Pulling myself to a sitting position against a rock, I called to Ralph, a few yards away.

"Ralph, I've about had it."

"I'll go ahead and meet the porters. They should be along pretty soon."

"O.K.," I answered. I was disappointed that my voice sounded so dead of spirit.

For perhaps a minute I could hear Ralph kicking along, and then the intense soundless night swept over me.

I pulled my flashlight out of my pack and placed it beside me. I would turn it on with the approaching sounds of the porters. I fell asleep exhausted.

An explosion of Swahili voices awakened me. I was surrounded by the friendly black faces. They were concerned and sympathetic. Ifada handed me a cup of hot tea. I had never felt more saved.

"Where's Wade?" I asked.

Ralph explained that Wade had sent Ifada and most of the porters to Shark's Tooth Lava Tower, and had positioned himself with flashlight on the ridge near our camp to act as a "lighthouse" to direct us back by the most direct route.

After much expressive talking in Swahili, they hoisted me up, a man on each arm and leg, and tottered unstably along. Several yards convinced them that the method was impractical. They put me down.

After much talking, they placed their blankets on the ground. Ralph got the climbing rope out, and they laced it under and between the blanket. I held the excess rope coils in my lap. Each of the four porters had a piece of rope wrapped in a blanket to put across his shoulder. Once more they hoisted me up and proceeded to carry me through the most difficult rock- and boulder-strewn country. We traveled this way for some distance, punctuated with much grunting and verbal abrupt phrases and with frequent rests.

They tried to find a better method. More discussion ensued. One man squatted facing down the trail, and three others lifted me up with my thighs straddling his neck, my legs and feet dangling in front of him. I hooked my arms around the necks of porters on each side and everyone stood up. A fourth man traveled behind, occasionally supporting my dangling head or boosting my position with his head in my back. The men on the sides often held my arms, sometimes providing some painful wrenches in the shoulders, but now we moved much faster. I knew it was going to be an extremely uncomfortable way to travel, but I silently vowed not to complain.

For several hours our grunting party twisted up, over, and around big rocks, small rocks, ridges, and ravines—always accompanied by a continual murmur of Swahili. The mountain hovered over us, its snow-frosted slopes flooded with moonlight. The occasional rest stops seemed unbelievably good, but all too quickly I was lifted onto the shoulders and bumped away. Shivering and almost in shock, I tried to disconnect myself from my broken body, but with only limited success. Tugged this way and that, I maintained one goal—arrival at camp.

Several forevers later, we were able to see Wade's light on the final ridge. More pushing, pulling, up and down brought us to camp. Trudging past our tent, they deposited me under the overhang beside a small campfire. It was about 11:30 p.m. They had been carrying me for four and a half hours.

Ifada began unlacing my boots. I set my teeth. A large pan on the edge of the fire threw out a thin mist of steam. The fireside seemed surrounded by curious eyes with an occasional glistening face catching the light. Holding my bare, swollen, bluish foot in his lap, he fished a steaming rag out of the boiling pot and slapped it around my foot and ankle. He then manipulated the foot vigorously in all directions. I continued to set my teeth. My mouth opened slightly but I didn't say anything. My pupils dilated. He performed the same rites on the other foot, and finished by rubbing an oily substance on both feet which he had melted onto his hands over the fire. A porter slipped my feet into my down boots, and another handed me a bowl of hot soup.

As I sipped the soup, I began telling myself that this unorthodox treatment would perhaps effect some miraculous cure. Finishing the soup, I handed off the empty bowl, thanked the men, said goodnight, and tried to stand up. I collapsed in an unceremonious heap and began shivering uncontrollably. Two porters carried me in sitting position to the tent. I crawled inside, and between waves of shaking, took off my wet wind pants and squirmed into my sleeping bag. I fell asleep quickly, still shivering.

23 ▲
MOUNTAIN RESCUE

GROANING MY WAY into the reality that was morning, I opened my eyes to a gray dawn. I had been painfully jarred into wakefulness several times during the night, but otherwise had slept deeply. Wade slowly opened his sleep-laden eyelids. Ralph propped himself on one elbow, blinking repeatedly. Footsteps outside announced Ifada with the morning tea.

"How did you sleep, Gene?" Wade asked.

"O.K."

Ralph spoke. "We've got a real problem on our hands getting you out of here. I think there's an airport in Arusha, but I don't know if they have helicopters."

"There's an airport there," I affirmed.

Wade nodded in agreement, but added, "I don't even remember seeing any choppers in the Nairobi Airport."

"I don't either," Ralph added.

"There must be choppers in Nairobi," I said, "and since Nairobi is a mile high they should be jet choppers, since a regular helicopter can't hover much over five or six thousand feet."

I pulled out my guidebook to Mount Kilimanjaro and read from it: "Facilities exist for Mountain Rescue. If needed, it can be initiated through the Police (phone Nairobi 2475 or Moshi 2222)." Ralph made a note of the phone numbers. "These guys ought to be able to help," I added.

About an hour later the party was almost ready to move on down the valley. Two porters were to stay behind in the "cave" to bring me food and water. I twisted my way to the tent opening and watched as Ralph set up a landing area for the helicopter, marked by an aluminum "space blanket" and strips of luminous cloth I had brought along for wand markers.

Ralph crawled into the tent with a piece of paper and a pencil stub. "I better have your home phone number."

I wrote it down for him.

"Oh, and yes, your survey map of the mountain, so I can show the pilot your exact position."

I pulled it out of a pocket and gave it to him.

"Gene, this rescue is liable to be pretty costly. We may have to get a helicopter from some farflung American air base; I don't know. How much are you willing to spend?"

"Look, Ralph, spend whatever is necessary to get me out of here. Maybe the American Embassy in Dar es Salaam can help locate an airplane."

"Since you talked to Senator Magnuson about this trip, maybe I can tell them you're a personal friend of his."

"Tell them I'm his brother if it'll help."

I felt vaguely discontent. Ralph packed up everything I didn't need. He was going to take it down so that there would be less load in the airplane.

It was almost 10 a.m. when Ifada and a few of the porters came to the tent to shake my hand. "I go straight out, Bwana. No rest. No sleep. Straight out. Get help."

"Thanks, Ifada. You're a good man and a good friend."

Ralph and Wade said good-by, and Ralph left a candy bar with me. They joined the line of porters and slowly descended down the valley. I watched as the last man passed from view. A heavy mixture of fog and gloom settled over my tent.

I twisted onto my side to get at the pockets of my pack. I decided to inventory my belongings to help pass the time. Thrusting a hand into a side pocket, I came up with a sturdy, metal ice screw. I held it in front of me and looked at it hard and curiously. Why hadn't I used one to anchor us before the accident? The more I pondered, the more interested I became in an answer. We had limited time, and placing screws would use too much of it. Not a good reason, I thought. I knew that the slope was too steep and rock-hard icy to allow a self-arrest. That would be reason enough to anchor us. But, I hadn't. Wade was damned worried. That too would be reason enough. But, I wasn't having trouble. That's no reason. Ralph was fatigued and slipping. Another pressing reason! But I hadn't secured us. It was disagreeable to think about. My mind tried to turn to other thoughts. Something inside wanted answers, and dragged my thoughts back. Neither Ralph nor Wade had suggested using the ice screws. Interesting, but still I was the leader.

I began adding the events leading to the accident. The seventy mile-five day climb of Kilimanjaro by the usual route had taken something out of me, and had left me with sunburn, blisters, and aching joints. The planned day of rest had turned into a frantic scramble of a day trying to find maps, porters, and a guide. The plod through the jungle with worry about route, the porter unrest, the ticks, these things had frayed a few edges. Our nutrition hadn't been all that good, what with the maggots on the meat, mosquito larvae in the water, and the advancing dehydration of altitude compounded by my diarrhea the night and morning of our final assault.

I felt that I was reaching some sort of an answer. Start with a fatigued body, add a worried mind, inject a few fears, compound the problem with the cold, the dehydration, and the hypoxia of altitude, and then call for a critical decision. It was clear. My judgment had disintegrated. I threw the ice screw back into the pack. I'd inventory some other time.

Rain spattering the tent with hundreds of minute thumps awakened me. Rivulets were flowing in the tent and some puddles were forming. The tent was windproof but not waterproof. It was imperative to keep dry because a soggy sleeping bag would offer no protection against the freezing night. I began sponging up the water with a wad of toilet paper, squeezing it into a cup. Some rivulets I could direct into a corner puddle which I stayed clear of, and bailed at my leisure. It was like being in a leaky life raft.

The chances of an aircraft arriving by morning were nil, and since the weather on this side of the mountain routinely closed in by noon, I probably couldn't expect help by the next evening either. More likely the day after that.

I welcomed the evening cold because the rain problem was solved. A light snow began to fall. A scuffling outside the tent indicated supper arriving.

"Bwana, food."

A plateful of cold meat and rice was passed into the tent. I forced myself to eat as much as I could, but was unable to finish.

Rummaging in my first aid kit, I found two aspirin, a half grain of codeine, and a sleeping pill. I swallowed them down and slept.

I awoke at dawn, about 6 a.m. Shortly thereafter I was surprised by the wild chirping of a single bird outside the tent. I didn't know we had any up here. Perhaps he feels the same way about me.

"Food, Bwana."

It was the other porter. Apparently they took turns bringing me food. He handed me a cup of black coffee. The tea was gone. I tasted it. It was awful but I drank it anyway. The bread and margarine were full of grit. I had a few bites. The blob of porridge was cold, gritty, and without milk or sugar. I ate it.

The tent and everything in it was getting damp. I hoped for a sunny day to dry things out.

At 8 a.m. I heard an airplane. I knew it was too soon to be for me, but somehow it filled me with hope anyway. The sound was quickly replaced by the wind rippling along the edge of the tent. Leaning on an elbow, I looked through the flapping tent opening. The plains of Africa spread before me for hundreds of miles.

I dozed off and on through the morning, and awoke to imagined airplanes frequently. By 1 p.m. the clouds were sweeping up the valley, snuffing out any chance of getting out by aircraft for another day.

Still no lunch by 2 p.m. A hail storm moved in and pummeled the tent. Anyway, it was better than rain.

A new worry began creeping into my consciousness. The tent was slanted somewhat downhill. With my legs extended downward and not moving much because of the pain, with the swollen ankles and altitude-thickened blood, I was beginning to worry about developing a thrombophlebitis in my legs, which could conceivably toss emboli to my lungs. I started a routine of exercising. Periodically I tried flexing my calf muscles and propping up my legs to improve venous circulation.

At 5 p.m there was still no lunch. I turned end for end and crawled out the tent opening. I waved my empty water bottle at the porters sitting at the edge of the overhang a hundred feet away. One of them came down.

"Water," I said, shaking my empty water bottle.

He nodded.

"Food?" I asked.

"No more food, Bwana."

Well, that explains that, I thought. From now on I can add hunger to my list of growing annoyances. When he returned with the water, I gave him two slices of bread with some margarine left over from breakfast.

By 7 p.m. the cloud level was below me at about eight thousand feet. Upward it was clear all the way to the faint stars beginning to appear. I began to think that this would be an ideal time to lift me out of here. They should have reached "civilization" easily by noon today. They have now had seven hours to secure a helicopter. But it now seems more likely that there will be no airplane. Tomorrow morning they'll start in on foot with a rescue party; it'll be two more days before they reach me; two more days without food.

I opened my eyes. It was morning. Light filtered through the top of the tent. A drop fell from the tent wall on my cheek and I wiped it away. Everything was rocky and gray as usual. As I awakened I slowly took stock of my situation.

This'll be the fourth day I've lain injured on this mountain, and the second day without food. The ground party should arrive by tomorrow evening, but what if they don't? I began to think of what things could prevent their returning. An accident on the way down with Wade and Ralph injured—but then Ifada would somehow get help to me, unless he was injured too. An automobile accident, that could do it. We had come upon a head-on collision on our trip from Nairobi. A Frenchman had been hopelessly crushed into the wreckage, and had died before we could even unsnarl him. And then, perhaps there are no helicopters in East Africa, and mounting an adequate rescue could be very difficult.

It became clear that after a reasonable period of time I had better start crawling my way out. It was an extremely bitter thought, but I wasn't going to lie up there and die while I still had some strength. Again I went over my estimates of when they got off the mountain, and how much time it could take to initiate a rescue. I came to a decision. If they didn't arrive by the next evening, I'd start crawling the following morning. Let's see. It took two days to walk up here, so it would probably take about five to crawl out. That'd be nine days after the accident. Men have survived far more. I'll make it. I'd better send the porters down tomorrow. No use dragging them down the drain with me. Poor devils, I know they're cold, hungry, and miserable. One of them was so grateful yesterday when I gave him my wool balaclava. It had accompanied me to Mount McKinley and Mount Aconcagua, and this was as good a way to part with it as any.

Haven't experienced much hunger or hunger pains, but I did have a lovely dream yesterday in which I consumed a large dinner, and a few minutes ago I smelled meat cooking. But then, I can also conjure up an airplane any time by just listening intently.

It was almost noon. I had been looking forward to this hour all morning. I was about to consume the candy bar that Ralph had left for me. Very carefully I removed the paper so as not to lose a crumb. I savored the paper, smelling the goodness out of it. Laying flat on my back, I held the candy over my face and opened my mouth widely, so that fragments of nuts or chocolate would not be lost. I took a bite and allowed the piece to be completely dissolved and swallowed before contemplating another bite. Thirty minutes later I licked the last from my lips and inhaled the odors from the paper once more before discarding it.

The sun was shining. Crawling out of my sleeping bag, I decided to allow it to air. I pushed the bag out the tent opening and crouched beside it. The warmth of the sun felt enormously good. I basked there until the discomfort of my position overpowered the comfort of the sun, then crawled back into the tent to stretch out, but carried several pebbles with me. I lined them up on the floor and proceeded to invent a game I dubbed "Kilimanjaro Stones." Boredom was becoming another enemy.

At 2 p.m. I was startled by what sounded like a faint shout from down in the valley. I instantly sat up and thought I heard another. Listening intently, I heard nothing more. If there had really been something, the porters would have heard it too, I reasoned. Imagination again. I flopped down. Perhaps five minutes went by.

But then I heard another shout from below. I sat up and scrambled to the tent opening. Another shout! I called wildly to the porters.

"Listen, listen!"

The porters didn't answer.

Another distant shout! This time the porters heard and began shouting themselves.

"They've come, they've come," I kept saying, mostly to myself.

Now I could see them slowly climbing up the valley.

As they got closer and closer I recognized John Wynne in the front of the column. John, at twenty our youngest member, had been with us on the conventional route up the mountain, but influenza had struck him from this ascent.

I pulled myself to a sitting position at the tent entrance and waited. John pantingly quickened his slow pace for the last several yards.

"How are you, Gene?"

"A lot better now, thank you."

"Here, I've got your mail." He produced a brown envelope from his pocket. "Highest mail delivery in Africa."

John was a member of the U.S. Postal Service and carried a picture of "Mr. Zip" on the back of his pack along with the American Flag that we had all sewn on our packs.

Eagerly I tore open the letter addressed to me in care of the Kibo Hotel, Private Bag, Moshi. It was from the Kilimanjaro Mountain Club.

Dear Sir,

I have been unable to find out any up-to-date information about the state of the track into Shark's Tooth Lava Tower. I am sorry to be so unhelpful.

I enclose a receipt for $2.82 and a membership card and book of rules.

> Yours truly,
> E. Forrest, Secretary
> Kilimanjaro Mountain Club

A few minutes later Wade trudged up. "How ya doin'?"

"It was beginning to get a little hungry up here."

Paul Robisch, another would-be member of our ascent who developed pulmonary edema at seventeen thousand feet on the standard route, then arrived with an Englishman named Mike Blandy.

Wade proceeded to fill me in on what had happened since they had left. They had hustled off the mountain in good time. Their rest stops had been short and infrequent. By early evening they crashed through the last wall of jungle and spilled into the trail-road. Wade and Ralph continued down the track until they came upon the house of an affluent villager with an old dilapidated truck. They quickly made a deal with him to take them to the nearest coffee plantation. He eagerly accepted, and the three of them bundled into the front of his truck, which took off down the dirt road with an incredible amount of snorting, clanging, and horn blowing.

They streaked down the rutted road, in the air almost as much as on the ground, throwing a huge trail of dust and distraught chickens out behind, and a swath of scurrying villagers out in front. The driver spoke, "Exciting, no?"

"Exciting, yes!" Wade shouted back at him. "Slow down." But the advice was lost to the din of the trip and glee of the driver.

Wheeling into the coffee plantation with a last few resounding bumps, the truck and driver reluctantly stopped.

"Thanks, I think," Wade said to the toothlessly grinning driver as he paid him off.

They were well received by the British landlords, fed bacon and eggs, and the phone calls began.

Several things gradually became evident over the next few hours. It was discovered that what few helicopters had existed in Tanzania and Kenya had left with the British when they had pulled out a few years previously. Next it was found that the Mountain Rescue Organization was severely handicapped by lack of experienced personnel and almost any kind of equipment. In fact, they had not brought out a living accident victim in five years, although they had brought out many bodies.

Wade and Ralph realized that the rescue would have to be effected by themselves, porters, and what isolated local individuals they could enlist. The next problem to confront them was that all the porters except Ifada and one young Chagga boy had dissolved into the villages. They did not have the slightest inclination to find themselves on the Umbwe Route again. We were never quite sure whether it was because of difficulty, fear, or superstition, but gone they were.

Ralph decided to stay in Moshi at the Livingstone Hotel, so that he would have access to telephone and telegraph communication, while Wade returned with Ifada to the Kibo Hotel to begin the process of recruiting new porters.

Ralph set up an office in the hotel lobby and began the process of notifying families, other members of our African Expedition, since all of us were going home together, and the American Embassy in Dar es Salaam. The Embassy informed him that there was one high altitude helicopter in East Africa working for an oil company down south somewhere. They said they would try to contact the company, but it might take several days before they could actually get the helicopter on the mountain, especially since there was a cyclone raging in northern Mozambique.

Ralph then arranged for an airplane to stand by at the Arusha airport to fly me to a hospital in Nairobi, if it seemed necessary when they got me off the mountain.

The next morning found Wade and Mrs. Breuhl attempting to put together a new group of porters, but with great difficulty since word as to the difficulties of the route had spread rapidly. Porters just would not go.

Mrs. Breuhl stomped her slippered feet, chanted her vehement mixture of German and Swahili, and marched in tight little circles, waving her index finger in admonishment. This, plus the promise of a bonus for each man, eliminated the objections, and one by one Mrs. Breuhl and Ifada picked the most dependable men for the mission.

To this group of porters was added John Wynne, Paul Robisch, and Mike Blandy. Mike, a biologist with the Tanganyika Coffee Research Station, was the only member of the Kilimanjaro Mountain Rescue Organization who could be mustered for this trip. They had headed for the mountain, and here they were.

"Where's Ifada?" I inquired.

"Snapping at the last porters in line," answered Wade.

Sure enough, there he was, bringing up the rear. He headed directly for me.

"How are you, Bwana?"

"Fine, Ifada."

He handed me an orange and two bananas. I devoured them immediately.

Under John's supervision two porters began reassembling a collapsible litter furnished by the rescue organization while the rest of the party struck camp. Mike informed me that he had talked to one of the natives in Swahili, and had discovered that there was an unmapped shelter about three or four miles away, a few thousand feet down. They had passed it on the way up, and it would be our goal today.

Finally they stretched out my sleeping bag, and I inched my way into it. Carefully they lifted me into the litter and strapped me in. I had not been this comfortable for days. With three men on each side, they slowly lifted the stretcher and began to move out. However, the natives seemed almost immediately discontent with the litter. Mumbling, groaning, and arguing surrounded me for about seventy-five yards, when they suddenly set me down. More Swahili arguing, and they began taking me out of the litter. They had decided to carry me on their shoulders as I had been carried days ago.

Again one porter squatted while they draped my legs over his shoulders. I hooked my arms around the necks of two more squatting natives, and they all stood up. The prospect of

facing a day and a half of this torture was a bitter disappointment. I hoped I didn't run out of lips to bite and teeth to
clench. But we were going down, and I reaffirmed my vow
not to complain.

The miles and hours dragged by slowly. As they plodded
along, my jacket became pushed up around my chest and
neck, exposing my bare abdomen to the chilling rain drops
now falling. My head bobbed on my neck, long since exhausted in trying to hold my head up. It can't be much farther,
I kept reassuring myself. Twice so far during the trip I had
let out uncontrollable moans. Both times it had been when the
forward porter had inadvertently run my dangling ankles
into boulders.

"There, Bwana."

I lifted my head and saw a prefabricated sheet metal hut a
hundred yards off the ridge.

By the time I crawled into the hut, I felt totally washed out.
Ifada began preparing supper. He went to great lengths to
provide a variety of vegetables and meat. I ate what I could,
but my appetite had disappeared. Sleep came quickly.

24 ▲
THE RETURN

WHILE CAMP WAS being cleared, I used boards, wire mesh, and tape to attempt to create "bombproof" splints for my ankles to better protect them for the day's journey.

We left at about 8 a.m. and began the tedious trip down. It was grueling and hazardous on top of the porters, but the porters were right. It was probably quicker than any other available way. The more dangerous areas were marked by utterances of the porters of, "Poli, poli," which I took to mean "careful," "look out," "I'm sorry," and/or "I think I'm going to drop him."

The hours scuffed by. Stunted trees began to appear, and I knew we had reached timber line. A short distance later, plants were in evidence and I could smell the odors of pollens. I had forgotten how much I had missed the green smell. Finally I could feel the genuine warmth of the earth flowing up to me, and there were flowers. We were beginning to enter steep forest; jungle would soon follow.

I blew away a fly buzzing in my face. We had been lucky as far as insect attacks were concerned. True, I had been immunized against most of the serious diseases of the world—smallpox, cholera, yellow fever, typhoid, paratyphoid, diphtheria, pertussis, tetanus, typhus, polio, and Rocky Mountain Spotted Fever—some of which were carried by insects, and we were taking malarial preventatives, but still the insects can wage an incredibly annoying war. There was no protection from the painful bites of the tsetse fly, which sometimes imparts the trypanosome parasite causing sleeping sickness. I had heard of the Congo floor maggot that crawls from the dust or cracks inside native huts to suck the blood of persons sleeping on the ground, and of the African tumbu fly, whose maggot larva burrows just beneath the skin producing a boillike inflammation.

By noon we were at ninety-four hundred feet, the site of our first night's camp. I remembered the mosquito larvae in the water. They were still there. We spent an hour resting and eating lunch. I forced myself to eat.

Mike explained that he had made arrangements for a couple of his companions from the coffee plantation to drive up the road in Land Rovers to meet us. This would save us several miles of trail walking.

After lunch I was thrust onto the porter's shoulders again, and the torture resumed. Every hour was taking a little more out of me. My back, neck, shoulders, legs ached unbearably. We continued nonstop for two hours and I almost couldn't take it. I hated to call a halt, but was on the verge when a cliff dropped off before us and they set me down.

"Better lower him in the litter," Wade advised.

All agreed. I was lifted into the litter and belays were arranged. It was a wonderful and rejuvenating break. At the bottom of the cliff I was once more hoisted onto the shoulders, and they started off.

"Doing O.K. up there?" Wade asked.

"At least I don't have to worry much about snakes," I managed to quip.

We were traveling a ridge now and I could faintly distinguish buildings far in the valley below—a new landmark in progress. It cheered me.

My bare abdomen was now exposed to the hot African sun. It occurred to me that I was a great target not only for sunburn but also for bird droppings. My spirit was up or down depending on how long they carried me without a stop. It was beginning to deteriorate again. At times I developed the peculiar feeling that the natives were carrying me off in some mysterious rite which culminated in tossing me over a cliff. We came to the cliff edge. They set me down again, and the litter was once more put together.

Another restful episode of belays, shouts, and lowerings brought me to the bottom and back onto the waiting shoulders. I knew we must be making spectacular time.

At 3:50 p.m. we crashed out of the jungle underbrush with the natives chanting "Rover, Rover," over and over again. They deposited me in the road and a drenching rain spilled onto us. I huddled under the overturned litter while the rest of our crew sat in the rain.

An hour and a quarter later, we could hear the four-wheel-drive Rovers grinding their way up the steep dirt road. Everyone cheered as the first of the Rovers came into view. The deeply tanned driver, with a very British handlebar mustache, leaned out the window and beamed at me, "Hi, Yank!" I felt proud.

Actually, as it turned out, this gentleman was named Nick Emmanuel and was of Greek ancestry. He was the owner of a large plantation and the chairman of the Kilimanjaro Mountain Rescue Group.

They helped me into the back of one of the Rovers, and we rocked and bumped our way down the mountain road. In about a half hour we arrived at the first houses. A native policeman with pith helmet, khaki shorts, and bush jacket stood at the edge of the road with his hand raised in an official halt. We ground to a stop. He spoke Swahili to Nick in the front of the vehicle. Nick answered and accepted a pencil and paper which he passed back to me.

"He wants your name for the records."

I wrote my name, and anticipating the next request, wrote my address also. Nick handed it back to him, and he gave Nick a small package wrapped in a piece of newspaper, along with several words in Swahili. Nick passed it back to me.

"Medicine for the injured man."

I unwrapped the parcel and found a small handful of large white tablets.

"Ask him what they are?"

An exchange of Swahili followed.

"Malaria," Nick smiled.

"Malaria?" I asked. "Didn't even know that was my problem."

Nick explained, "The capacity to issue medicine was one of the characteristics of British government that had impressed these people before their independence. Doesn't matter what the illness or injury is, you get whatever medicine they happen to have."

We bumped onward.

The Coffee Research Station with its perfectly groomed gardens and lawns was a delight to see. We cruised up the winding driveways for a half mile or more before stopping in front of a yellow stucco home. All except myself jumped out of the Rovers. Some sat on the lawn, some stretched and yawned, some milled about, but all were glad to be off the mountain. Beer bottle caps popped around me, and I was offered a pint-sized bottle of Tusker Beer. Days without much food had done nothing to improve my stomach. It sounded much better than it tasted.

Ralph came running from a newly arrived car and threw his arms around me. We hugged each other like a couple of long lost brothers. It was very good to see him again.

The home and beer belonged to coffee botanist Mike Biggers and his wife Jeri, who were becoming concerned about getting me to a hospital. Nick commandeered a local bus and dispatched the porters to Marangu village. Ralph, both Mikes, and myself headed for the German Lutheran Missionary Hospital in the village of Chame.

Mike Biggers explained that the government-run public hospitals left much to be desired, and besides he knew the chief surgeon at this hospital.

Darkness had fallen heavily onto the village by the time we

got there. We parked in front of the hospital while Biggers walked up the road to the nearby home of the surgeon. He returned in about twenty minutes.

"Afraid we've got a bit of a problem, chaps. My surgeon friend is on holiday. However, there is a German doctor and an African doctor here. Let's see what they can do."

I agreed.

The next problem was that the x-ray room was locked up. We drove to the housekeeper's home and got the key. They carried me up the hospital stairs and into the x-ray department.

Next, it developed that the x-ray technician was gone and no one knew how to operate the machine. After considerable discussion and consultation with the direction manual, the physicians announced that they were quite sure they could take the films, but equally sure that they couldn't develop them. Biggers spoke up.

"I do a lot of photography in my botanical work. I wouldn't mind having a go at it. Let's have a look at the darkroom."

The pictures were taken and Mike went into the darkroom. Several minutes later he emerged with a broad smile and some rather decent films, which he ceremoniously hung on the view box. I peered between the several heads gathered in front of the films. The left ankle film showed the distal end of the fibula broken off in the joint. The right ankle film revealed very little since the picture had pretty well missed the ankle.

"Well, I know one is broken anyway," I said.

They lifted me onto a low-wheeled cart, and we headed for the cast room. We decided to put a circular cast on the broken one and a plaster splint on the questionable one, since both seemed equally swollen, blue, and painful. I felt enormously improved with casts on my legs. I had been waiting five days for this relief.

Mike had invited us to spend the night with him. After supper I decided to take a bath, which was a pretty exciting affair with both legs in plaster. They ended up outside the tub, with the rest of me submerged and spouting water.

My night was plagued with mosquitoes and episodes of diarrhea. By morning there were several trails of plaster from my bedroom to the toilet.

After breakfast Mike presented me with a pair of home-made crutches. Nothing could have been more welcome; I was now off the floor at last. This is especially pleasant in Africa, where you never know what you might come face to face with while crawling.

Mike Blandy stopped by to join us for a cup of coffee. Good-bys and thank yous were said, and Blandy proceeded to drive us up to the Kibo Hotel.

I hobbled down the hotel walk on my crutches, and was met with great enthusiasm and welcome by a tearful Mrs. Breuhl and a smiling Ifada.

I sat at the table in the hotel lounge, where I had sat with Ifada something over a week ago. Each native porter filed past me shaking my hand and offering expressions and gestures far more meaningful than the Swahili I didn't understand.

25

DAY FIFTY-ONE

SIX WEEKS LATER I was sitting in the office of an orthopedic surgeon in my home town. He had just removed my cast and had my ankle x-rayed. I was awaiting his return from the x-ray department to give me his verdict as to the completeness of healing.

My mind flashed over the events since saying good-bys in the Kibo Hotel. I had returned to Nairobi for a celebration dinner and interviews by the press, then on to Copenhagen overnight, and back to Seattle. Somehow my adventure had sparked much imagination and excitement, and we arrived in Seattle to a greeting of television cameras, journalists, officials, family, and friends. My ankles had been re-x-rayed, revealing that only the left one had been broken. A new cast had been applied. After a week at home I had gone back to my medical practice on crutches. The weeks had gone by rapidly, inconveniently, and often painfully. My daydream was broken by the return of the surgeon. He had a perplexed look.

"Gene, I'm afraid your ankle isn't healing quite right. You've developed a non-union. Apparently the injury was so violent that you tore the periosteum from the distal fragment. There's just not enough circulation to grow bone."

"What do you suggest, Bill?"

"Well, I doubt if leaving the cast on any longer will help. We could operate it, but I can't really give you any assurance that it will end up any better than what you might develop with a fibrous union. I suggest we wait for six months or longer, and see how you do. We can always operate then."

I thanked him and left. As I limped along the sidewalk a blowing piece of newspaper curled around my leg; I nudged it loose with my cane and it blew into the street, where the passing traffic tore it to bits. There seemed to be a lot of traffic for a Wednesday afternoon—roaring engines, squealing tires, and exhaust fumes. I stood on the corner waiting for the traffic light to change. A policeman stood on the corner across the street. There were no cars coming now, and I would have crossed except I knew if I did the policeman would give me a ticket or a lecture or both. I had to wait for the machine to tell man when he could move. The distant Cascade Mountains were obscured by a thick bluish smoke haze, and I could smell the offensive odor from the pulp mills. A far-off siren whined its way to someone's tragedy.

The stoplight changed. I didn't move. I just stood there wondering if I would ever climb another mountain.

Epilogue

THERE IS AN old saying—"Time heals all wounds", but anyone who has sustained a severe wound knows that this is not true. Nevertheless, while time may not heal the wound, the passage of time does allow man to endure, cope with, and even accept his injury as just another chink in the armor.

Time did not heal my broken bone, but as months passed and scar tissue developed around the unmended bone ends, I began to learn what things I could and could not do, and began trying to push those of category two into category one.

The things I couldn't do I promised myself I would be able to do next month, the month after, or maybe next year. While I convalesced I had considerable time to write, plan, and even to dream. With the summits of North America, South America, and Africa behind me, I looked toward Europe.

The highest peak on the Continent of Europe does not lie in Switzerland as one might suspect, but lies in the extreme eastern edge of the Continent near the Black Sea. This peak, Mount Elbrus, 18,480 feet, rises in the Caucasus Mountains in the Georgian Republic of Russia. The Georgian Republic is famous as the birthplace of Stalin, but more intrigue surrounds the area in its role as the legendary origin of the Caucasian Race. In the villages of the Caucasus the mountain people live to be well over 100 years of age. Their secret of longevity has defied even the most intense scientific investigation.

Some study and a few inquiries followed by quite a few letters found me in touch with the Honorable Secretary for Foreign Relations of the Mountaineering Federation of the U.S.S.R., Eugene Gippenreiter. He detailed some of my potential problems. "It is characteristic of this area that one feels the effects of altitude much stronger than elsewhere, mainly, vomiting, headache, and weakness. Even my friend Tenzing Norgay, a hero of Everest, felt sick when we attempted to climb this mountain in March 1963!"

It was the Fall of 1968. I convinced myself I would be ready by the Summer of 1969. A group of climbers were put together and I went into training. By the Spring of 1969 I realized that in spite of my enthusiasm there were certain essential things that my ankle would not yet do. With bitter regret I called off the expedition.

Seventeen months after my tumble down Kilimanjaro, I successfully climbed a summit, Mount Shuksan in Washington, an interesting combination of rock, ice, snow and glaciers. I had climbed the mountain before, many years ago, but this time as I stood on the peak I felt a quiet exuberance. Reaching this summit represented considerably more to me than just another peak. It was a special victory. For a long time I looked intently at the rugged spires of lesser summits poking through the swirling clouds below. I knew I was ready to challenge Mount Elbrus, the summit of Europe, in 1970.

▲

This
book was
composed in
11 point Janson
linotype, a typeface
issued by Anton Janson
in the seventeenth century.

Design by Linda Purnell